CODE
TO JOY

The Four-Step Solution to

Unlocking Your Natural

State of Happiness

George Pratt, Ph.D., and Peter Lambrou, Ph.D.
with John David Mann

Harper

An Imprint of Harpe

D0348765

HarperOne

This book contains advice and information relating to health care. It is not intended to replace medical advice and should be used to supplement rather than replace regular care by your doctor. It is recommended that you seek your physician's advice before embarking on any medical program or treatment. All efforts have been made to assure the accuracy of the information contained in this book as of the date of publication. The publisher and the authors disclaim liability for any medical outcomes that may occur as a result of applying the methods suggested in this book. The individual experiences recounted in this book are true. However, the names and certain descriptive details have been changed to protect the identities of those involved.

The lines from "What Do You Do with the Mad That You Feel?" are the copyright of Fred M. Rogers, and are used with permission from the Fred Rogers Company.

CODE TO JOY: *The Four-Step Solution to Unlocking Your Natural State of Happiness.* Copyright © 2012 by George Pratt, Ph.D., and Peter Lambrou, Ph.D. All rights reserved. Printed in the United States of America. No part of this book may be used or reproduced in any manner whatsoever without written permission except in the case of brief quotations embodied in critical articles and reviews. For information address HarperCollins Publishers, 10 East 53rd Street, New York, NY 10022.

HarperCollins books may be purchased for educational, business, or sales promotional use. For information please e-mail the Special Markets Department at SPsales@harpercollins.com.

HarperCollins website: http://www.harpercollins.com

HarperCollins®, ≜®, and HarperOne™ are trademarks of HarperCollins Publishers.

Design by Level C
Illustrations by Dwight Been

FIRST HARPERCOLLINS PAPERBACK EDITION PUBLISHED IN 2013

Library of Congress Cataloging-in-Publication Data
Pratt, George J.
Code to joy : the four-step solution to unlocking your natural state of happiness / George Pratt, Peter Lambrou, with John David Mann. — 1st ed.
p. cm.
Includes bibliographical references.
ISBN 978–0–06–205941–3
1. Happiness. 2. Joy. 3. Positive psychology. 4. Self-actualization (Psychology) I. Lambrou, Peter T. II. Mann, John David. III. Title.
BF575.H27P735 2012
158.1—dc23 2011024396

13 14 15 16 17 RRD(H) 10 9 8 7 6 5 4 3 2 1

CONTENTS

FOREWORD

THE TWENTIETH CENTURY HAD its share of medical miracles. I should know. When you've survived a heart attack, had quintuple bypass surgery, and you're still going strong a quarter-century later, it gives you a pretty healthy appreciation for modern medicine.

Still, there are some aspects of the human condition medicine can't touch. Or at least it couldn't until now. Modern medicine has made us a lot healthier—but what about *happier?* That may be where the frontier of medicine lies in this still young century. And one of the undisputed masters of that new frontier is a clinical psychologist named George Pratt.

The first time I met Dr. Pratt he was a guest on *Larry King Live*, talking about a fascinating approach to healing our emotions and creating lasting improvements in our productivity and sense of fulfillment.

"Whether it's an unresolved hurt, persistent low self-esteem, or vague sense of anxious unease," said Dr. Pratt, "most of us struggle with some version of what we call *the fog of distress.* It clouds our lives, interfering with our relationships, our careers, even our health. And no matter how many hours you spend on the couch, talking it through just doesn't always do it."

Why not?

"Because there's typically a disconnect," he explained, "between what we logically know about ourselves and the place in the brain where our emotions live. Sometimes you just can't get there from here. You have to find alternative ways to get that information to click."

Alternative ways like what? Like *energy psychology.*

If you've never heard the term before, you're not alone. Neither had I, before that show. But in the years to come, you and I will be hearing about it plenty. It refers to innovative techniques that affect the body's energy systems, almost like a 60,000-mile tune-up of the thoughts and emotions. Using these techniques, as my distinguished guest explained it, you can clear out the past traumas and events that created those disconnects in the first place. The result? It's something like what happens when a fresh wind blows away the clouds: *the sun comes out.*

"Actually," he added, "it's a pretty easy thing to do. And it works."

Dr. Pratt has helped pro golfers and ballplayers improve their game, jilted young men and women get over heartbreak, estranged couples get their groove back. He has helped people get past the trauma of terrible accidents, restart faltering careers, recover lost self-confidence, and move past irrational fears.

He has even helped one talk show host I know—me.

Even before we had him on the show that first time, I knew a little bit about the good doctor. He had worked with two people on the *Larry King Live* staff, and they had gotten fabulous results from those sessions. Soon I had him on as a guest again, and this time he talked about "creating your own joy."

Now I was *really* intrigued.

We set up a time when he could give me a private demonstration of the approach you're about to explore in this book. So we'd have something to work with, I described an emotional issue in my own life. What he did with it in the fifteen minutes we spent together blew my mind. To say it was impressive would be a crime of understatement. It was *remarkable*. When he says it's a simple and easy process, he's not kidding. When he says *it works,* he's not kidding there either.

George Pratt is a true modern-day healer, and what he and his colleague, Dr. Peter Lambrou, have created in the pages you're about to read is a brilliant formula for tapping into our highest potential. I predict it will change many people's lives for the better.

Including yours.

Whatever is going on in your life, whatever is keeping you from being as successful, as productive, as flat-out *joyful* as you'd like to be, there's a path that will take you there. I know, because I've experienced it firsthand.

Larry King

INTRODUCTION

Stefanie's Question

Something is not right.
—Miss Clavel, in the middle of the night, in *Madeline*

A FEW YEARS AGO a woman named Stefanie came to our office seeking treatment. In the course of our first visit, she asked us a question she had been trying to answer for decades. It's a question millions of people have asked throughout history. Maybe you have asked it yourself.

Stefanie's history, we soon learned, was a rags-to-riches success story. Growing up in a poor family, she took a job in her teens as an office assistant for an advertising company. Working her way up through the ranks, she eventually reached the top, so that by her mid-forties she had become CEO and majority owner of the firm. Stefanie also had a rich personal life. A kind and generous woman, she was active in the community where she lived with her husband, proud parents of two healthy, thriving kids.

In fact, Stefanie appeared to have been living a charmed life in every way—except for one thing: she was deeply unhappy.

Stefanie's unhappiness was practically tangible. When she entered the room, it was as if a dark cloud entered with her. As she began describing her situation, it became clear that this dark cloud followed her into every corner of her life.

By all accounts she was a great mother, but she didn't *feel* like a great mother. She also felt deeply guilty about the collapse of a previous marriage many years earlier, and that guilt hovered over her like the gloom of an overcast sky. Her health was affected, too: now in her fifties, Stefanie was having severe stomach and digestive problems and had recently undergone back surgery for a bad disc. Despite all her successes, that dark cloud had also cast its shadow over her professional world. After a series of management mishaps, Stefanie's advertising company had recently slipped into bankruptcy.

For no apparent reason, Stefanie's life was unraveling.

"I've seen psychiatrists here in California," she said, "and in New York, and in London. I've been on every antidepressant. I've read all the books and articles about mood issues. I've read everything and tried everything, but that unhappiness still persists—and I don't know why. Everyone tells me I have nothing to complain about and everything to be grateful for. And I know they're right. But knowing that doesn't make it better."

And then Stefanie asked The Question:

"Why aren't I happy?"

Over the course of our sixty years of combined clinical practice, we have heard thousands of variations of Stefanie's question, from thousands of people:

Why am I anxious? nervous? insecure? always worried? Why can't I seem to find or sustain a fulfilling relationship? find work I enjoy? relax when I am at home with my family? Why do I have this irrational fear of crowds . . . of men . . . of women . . . of elevators . . . of food . . . of closed spaces . . . of open spaces . . . of being alone . . . of being with others? Why can't I get over that breakup? my compulsive behavior? my challenges with money? my feeling that I'm a fraud?

In a million different versions, Stefanie's question echoes throughout our society and within virtually everyone we know. You probably have your own version.

We are the healthiest, best nourished, and longest-living generation in history. By all rights, we ought to be the happiest, most purposeful, productive, and fulfilled generation in history, too. But for some reason, we're not.

Why not?

It's a puzzle we've been pursuing for decades—and the answer turns out to have something to do with how water turns into fog.

IMAGINE YOU ARE STANDING just outside your home, surrounded by a dense fog, so thick you can't see the other side of the street in front of you. You look to the right, then to the left, but you cannot see more than fifty feet in any direction. You are surrounded.

How much water do you suppose it takes to create that blanket of fog that has completely isolated you from your world?

Before you read on, think about this for a moment. Don't worry if you're not good at math or have no background in physics. Just take a commonsense guess. How much water do you think it took to create this fog that surrounds you?

Now, are you ready for the answer? *A few ounces.* The total volume of water in a blanket of fog one acre around and one meter deep would not quite fill an ordinary drinking glass.

How is this possible? First the water evaporates, and the resulting vapor then condenses into minuscule droplets that permeate the air. In that one-acre block of fog, one drinking glass's worth of water disperses as some *400 billion tiny droplets* suspended in the air, creating an impenetrable cloak that shuts out light and makes you shiver.

This is exactly what happens with certain painful or difficult experiences.

Human beings are remarkably adaptable. Most of the time, when negative events occur, we are able to learn from them, shrug them off, and go on with our lives. The experience simply evaporates, leaving us a bit older and wiser. But not always. Sometimes, especially when we are very young, we have experiences that we cannot shake. Even if they seem insignificant, no more substantial than a glass of water, when these upsetting experiences evaporate, they then condense into billions of droplets of anger, fear, self-doubt, guilt, and other negative feelings, surrounding us with a suffocating blanket that suffuses every aspect of our lives for years to come.

We call this *the fog of distress.*

Typically, this vague sense of unease parks itself in the background, like the annoying hum of a refrigerator or air conditioner we have learned to block out from our conscious awareness. But whether we are aware of it or not, it pervades our existence like an insistent headache, interfering with our ability to have healthy relationships, to perform to our potential at work, or to have lives that are anywhere near as fulfilling as they could be. Over the years, that background hum can sabotage our careers, friendships, marriages. Sometimes, as with Stefanie, even our physical health starts to suffer.

What is this fog made of? It is part feelings and part beliefs, partly subconscious and partly bioelectrical. You can think of it as an interference pattern, like radio static, typically set up in the early years of childhood, when our defenses were still fairly unformed and we hadn't yet developed our adult, logical ways of thinking. In other words, it lies outside the domain of our conscious, logical, verbal thought process. It is like a computer program running in the background, shading our thoughts and feelings, reactions and behaviors, our view of ourselves and of our world—all largely without our conscious awareness that it is even there.

For some, this fog of distress shows up in very distinct and specific ways, such as an unshakable fear or irrational anxiety, a problem in one particular area of life. For others, like Stefanie, it is more vague and generalized. That is, it's not that any one specific thing is so terribly wrong. It's more that *nothing is quite right.*

This is why Stefanie's efforts hadn't given her any relief. Psychotherapeutic drugs, like antidepressants or anti-anxiety medications, cannot disperse that fog; at best, they can somewhat blunt its impact. Talking it over, whether with friends, counselors, or therapists, won't disperse it either, because it doesn't yield to reason and logical analysis. Trying to "talk it through" is like trying to reach an underwater cave by driving around the city streets. No matter how long you drive or which route you take, you won't get there. We have to get out of the car, get off the streets and into the water, and swim a different route altogether.

Fortunately, such a path exists. That's what this book is about.

THE WORST THING ABOUT this fog of distress is that it can be so persistent that we come to think of it as "normal." Yet it is *not* normal. We are designed with extraordinary capacities for growth, self-regulation, and self-healing. Our innate blueprint is beautifully crafted to produce a life of productivity, creativity, fulfillment, and joy. *We are meant to be happy.* Instinctively, we all know this, somewhere deep inside. We all know what it's like to feel a burst of delight. Every one of us has at some point in our lives experienced a sense of ecstatic joy, of euphoria at the sheer sensation of being alive.

Have you ever wondered why that experience has to be so rare and fleeting?

The answer is, *It doesn't.*

Our clinical experiences over the past few decades have shown us that it *is* possible to regain that sense of childlike delight at living and to live our lives to the fullest. As a result of this work, we have come to believe that we are all here on this earth to be happy and healthy, to experience joy, love, connection, and contribution. You *can* become a better, smarter, calmer, more focused, more powerful, and more deeply joyful *you*.

For that to happen, we need to address this pervasive fog of distress, understand where it comes from and how to dissipate it.

We have spent the past several decades unraveling this puzzle, using the tools of conventional psychology along with new methods and insights from the latest findings at the cutting edge of a field of research and therapy called *energy psychology*. Since we began exploring this new frontier in the 1980s, in our practices, workshops, and public demonstrations, we have administered more than 45,000 individual treatments, with remarkable and consistently reliable results.

Over the past decade, we have adapted our approach into a simple protocol that you can administer yourself. It is powerfully simple and effective. We have seen thousands of people use it to clear away their own fog of distress.

This is exactly what happened with Stefanie. In that first visit, we took her through the four steps of this simple protocol:

Step 1: Identify. First, looking back through her life, we helped Stefanie identify an early painful event whose impact had cast its long shadow into her world, along with the self-limiting beliefs her young mind had formed as a result of that experience.

In chapter 1, we take you through a simple, step-by-step process for doing the same thing. (We also reveal what the event was that had such an impact on Stefanie.) In chapter 2, we look at the most common self-limiting beliefs and how to identify them in yourself. In chapter 3, we explore where these beliefs reside and why they have such a firm grip on us and learn a fascinating method for flushing them to the surface where we can deal with them.

Step 2: Clear. Next, we worked with Stefanie using special breathing exercises and neuromuscular techniques to realign her body's natural electrical polarity and help disperse that pervasive fog.

In chapter 4, we explore the body's *biofield* and what happens when our electrical polarities become reversed or disordered. We also learn a set of techniques for realigning our electrical polarity, incorporating cognitive psychology together with elements from age-old disciplines, including yogic focus and acupressure.

Step 3: Repattern. Next, we helped Stefanie permanently release the self-limiting belief we identified in step 1 and then install an opposite, *empowering belief* into her being.

Chapter 5 explores the concept of *self-efficacy,* that is, the ability to step into the driver's seat and direct our own lives, together with fascinating new research findings on the power of mental imagery. In this chapter we also walk you through the *repattern* step, showing you how to create a new story for your life.

Step 4: Anchor. Finally, we showed Stefanie several powerful techniques for anchoring those new beliefs and thought patterns so they would become a permanent part of her and not simply a form of temporary relief.

In chapter 6 we show you how to complete this simple *anchoring* step and use it in the weeks and months ahead as a quick refresher, to ensure that the impact of the Four-Step Process stays with you. In chapter 7 we look at ways to use the Four-Step Process to unwrap further layers and tap into your full potential, and in chapter 8 we outline some additional simple, daily practices, drawn from our clinical experiences as well as the latest research, that will help you create the rich life you deserve.

These four steps—*identify, clear, repattern, anchor*—form the core of what you will learn in the pages of *Code to Joy.* In this book, we're going to show you what this process is, how and why it works, and how you can make it work for you.

By the time Stefanie left our office that day, the dark cloud was gone. That was several years ago. It has not returned.

CHAPTER ONE

An Interview with Yourself

What do you do with the mad that you feel
When you feel so mad you could bite?
When the whole wide world seems oh, so wrong . . .
And nothing you do seems very right?
—Fred Rogers, on *Mister Rogers' Neighborhood*

YOU ARE WALKING THROUGH a field, munching absentmindedly on a snack. The sun is out, the air is balmy. A light breeze at your back. Life is good.

Suddenly you hear an earthshaking crash.

Startled, you look up at the horizon just in time to see a gigantic plume of ash and dust volcanoing up into the sky and spreading out to form a gigantic cloud that will persist for days, weeks, perhaps years. It will blot out the sun and completely change your world. Chances are, you will not live to see it dissipate.

Oh, one more detail: you are a dinosaur.

SCIENTISTS TELL US IT was an asteroid striking Earth millions of years ago that caused the death of the dinosaurs. The impact threw so much debris into the atmosphere, they say, that it darkened the skies and transformed the climate into what is sometimes termed *nuclear winter*, so named because a similar effect would result from the explosion of a series of nuclear bombs.

The impact of traumatic personal events can have the same kind of effect, darkening the skies of our own outlook and causing a chilling effect that permeates every aspect of our lives.

To see how this happens, let's return for a moment to our first office visit with our client Stefanie, whom we met in the introduction.

Stefanie's First Quarter

One clue to the source of Stefanie's unhappiness surfaced within our first few minutes of conversation, when she described the nagging guilt she felt over the collapse of her first marriage. Though it had been many years since this happened, her feelings were as strong now as they had been then. In fact, in many ways they were stronger. The old saying "Time heals all wounds" could not be further from the truth. Wounds like Stefanie's don't get milder with age. They get worse, often digging deeper and deeper grooves in the psyche.

To Stefanie, that divorce was an asteroid strike. It may have happened in the distant past, but the debris it threw into the atmosphere still darkened her skies several decades later.

This is not purely psychological. Stefanie, remember, was already experiencing very real physiological symptoms, too, along with the gradual breakdown of her personal and professional lives. The impact of traumatic events in our lives records itself onto our being on many levels at once. We are talking about something that is physiological, emotional, and energetic, as well as psychological.

Sometimes the traumatic event seems as obvious as an actual asteroid hitting the planet. After all, it didn't take long before we were hearing about Stefanie's divorce. She spoke about it within the first few minutes of our meeting.

Other times, it is not so obvious. Often significant events occur in our lives, especially when we are very young and impressionable, that nobody around us notices at the time they occur. In fact, these early events can be so subtle that we ourselves don't notice them or realize the impact they have had.

This was the case with Stefanie. As we said, that nagging sense of guilt she described was one clue—but only one. Stefanie's unhappiness did not start there; the divorce itself only added to a cloud of debris that already existed within her and had existed for many years before that.

In the course of our conversation, Stefanie mentioned a number of events throughout her life that had had an impact on her. As we asked about her childhood, she had a sudden thought.

"I don't know if this is significant," she began. "Probably not . . ."

This is worth noting, by the way: when people preface a recalled event by saying, "I don't know if this really means anything," it almost always *does*.

We encouraged her to go on.

"Well, this one time, when I was seven, I helped my aunt move some furniture around one afternoon. When we were finished, she thanked me and paid me a quarter. I hadn't expected to be paid, and I was thrilled. It was the first money I'd ever earned." She shook her head slowly. "You know, I haven't thought about this for, oh, probably *decades*." She paused, letting the distant memory replay itself. "I was so proud. I couldn't wait to tell my family. I bolted home, ran inside, told my folks about it, and held up the quarter for them to see.

"They were shocked. 'What did you think you were doing?!' they hissed at me. 'You *never* take money from family!'

"I was crushed." She paused again, as if lost in the memory, then added, "I felt so humiliated."

Her parents no doubt meant well; they were only trying to pass on what they considered their good family values. But the message Stefanie took from the experience was fused into her being:

It's wrong and shameful to make money.

And now, a half century later, Stefanie had lost a successful company and was rapidly on her way to losing her health—out of lingering shame over a quarter.

How could such a seemingly minor event have such a deeply felt and long-lasting impact? To answer this, we need to look at the nature of trauma.

Tiny Event, Big Impact

Our modern word *trauma* is identical to the ancient Greek term for *wound*. When we speak of a trauma, we generally mean an event, either physical or psychological, that has wounded us severely, causing lasting harm or injury to our body and/or mind. Examples of trauma include such events as a car accident, serious injury, the death of someone close, a threat to our own life, an experience in a war zone, a major house fire. A traumatic event is one that wounds and leaves deep scars.

When a frightening or threatening event occurs, input from our sensory organs—the sights, sounds, and smells of danger—are transmitted directly to a pair of tiny, almond-shaped nerve clusters deep in the brain called *amygdalae*. The amygdalae immediately send alert messages to other parts of the brain that trigger the release of *glucocorticoids,* the fight-or-flight stress hormones such as cortisol and norepinephrine. (Bessel van der Kolk, M.D., perhaps the world's leading authority on trauma, describes the amygdalae as "the smoke detector of the brain.") Flooding the system, these hormones provide the muscles with an immediate burst of energy and at the same time shut down all nonessential processes, such as digestion and immune response. Meanwhile, the prefrontal cortex—the front part of the brain, where logic and rationality are based—goes dark, that is, it essentially shuts down.

Severe trauma can have profound and lasting damage, crippling one's ability to trust others and creating a deeply embedded array of symptoms known as post-traumatic stress disorder, or PTSD. These symptoms can include persistent and intrusive memories; nightmares or disturbed sleep; sudden and seemingly unprovoked outbursts of anger or other emotions; hypervigilance; and a degree of emotional numbness.

"But wait," you might be thinking. "Post-traumatic stress—from a scolding over a quarter? That seems a little extreme!"

Fair enough. From outward appearances, Stefanie's encounter with her parents' disapproval hardly seems to qualify as a bona fide trauma on a par with life-threatening violence or serious bodily injury. It's not as if she were beaten and thrown out of the house, or even punished. She suffered no physical harm. Even all these years later, sitting in our office and talking about it, Stefanie herself had a hard time crediting it as a very significant thing.

But it was. Whether or not anyone saw it happen, whether she herself was even consciously aware of it, an asteroid had slammed into young Stefanie's world, and the debris it threw into her atmosphere had never gone away. Even now, at the distance of a half-century, it still blocked the sun from shining in her sky.

We've used the Four-Step Process thousands of times with people who have experienced full-blown, major traumas, not just from childhood but also in their adult lives, and we'll share some of these remarkable stories of crisis and recovery in this book. But a precipitating event doesn't have to be dramatic or obviously traumatic to have a deep and lasting impact.

Remember, under the right circumstances, all it takes to create a blanket of impenetrable fog is a glassful of water. Stefanie's event does not qualify as what we would think of as a clinical trauma. Instead, it was something more insidious: a *microtrauma*.

A microtrauma is an event or experience that would seem from all outward appearances to be not a very big deal, and certainly not devastating. In fact, it may be so mild that you think you've completely put it behind you. But you haven't. It stays with you, just as Stefanie's memory had stayed with her so vividly that she was able to pull it up within minutes of our first meeting her, even though, by her own admission, she had not thought about it for decades.

This is why we say these microtraumatic events can be even more insidious than full-blown traumas: precisely *because* they hide behind the veneer of innocent insignificance. These are often the kinds of experiences that seem so trite, so harmless, that, looking back, we have a hard time seeing them as being significant turning points in our lives.

What's more, other people in our lives, especially those we look to as authorities, often dismiss such "insignificant" events as well, reinforcing our own sense that they should not have any real impact on us.

"Get over it," they say. "Don't be a baby. It's no big deal." And we believe them. "They're right," we tell ourselves. "It was nothing. Sure it happened, and so what? I got over that ages ago."

But it was *not* nothing. To us, it was an asteroid strike. And for most of us, it's not something you "get over." It's something that casts a suffocating blanket over the climate of your life—until you learn the simple tools it takes to identify it and clear it.

There is a reason we often don't realize the full impact of our own microtrauma. There is a natural tendency to dismiss it, to do our best to put it behind us and just get on with living. To an extent, this is a healthy, protective mechanism. We minimize the impact of what has happened in order to cope and go on. But sometimes, especially when we are young, we cannot simply "put it behind us." Instead, we can only drive it deeper inside, and the short-term gain in composure comes at the expense of long-term suffering.

"What do you do with the mad that you feel?" asked Fred Rogers in his popular children's television program *Mister Rogers' Neighborhood*. It's a great question. What *do* we do with the mad that we feel—the shame, the embarrassment, the fear, the panic, or the sadness?

The answer, typically, is that we don't do *anything* with it. It just stays there, like that choking dust cloud of debris that blocked out the sun and killed off the dinosaurs.

A Single Wave

As part of our annual seminar, we take the entire group into the ocean to swim with dolphins. One day, we were preparing to go into the water when one of the participants, a young woman named Alex, approached us and said, "I have a little problem. I can't go in with you—I'm afraid."

We assured her that the water would be calm, shallow, and not at all dangerous. There were no sharks anywhere in this vicinity.

"No, you don't understand," she said. "I'm not afraid of sharks, I'm afraid of the water. I mean, *severely* afraid."

All her life, she explained, she had been afraid of water—*so* afraid that she was unable to drink straight from a glass. If she wanted a drink of water, she would have to use a straw. She could take brief showers with some difficulty. But the only baths she could take were sponge baths, because she was unable to sit down in a tub of water.

Alex was there at the seminar with her dad, and as we briefly explained how early events can trigger deeply held limiting beliefs, he spoke up.

"If you're talking early events, I think I know exactly what it was for Alex."

They had been at the beach once when Alex was three years old. As they stepped carefully out into the surf, a small wave came up and surged over little Alex's head.

"I grabbed her and picked her up," he explained. "It was over in moments, and she was never in any danger. But she never wanted to go swimming after that."

The original event that generated Alex's sense of trauma had lasted all of ten seconds. Its impact had lasted two decades.

We took her through the Four-Step Process, right then and there. Once we'd finished she said, "Huh. That's weird."

What was weird? we asked.

"I feel different."

She asked her dad to get her a glass of water—and right in front of the entire group, she did something she had not done once in twenty years: she drank water from a glass. Later that day, she walked out into the surf and *waded in* up to her waist. It was an amazing thing to watch.

The next day, as we went out onto the open ocean, Alex followed along in a boat, nervous but excited. As the dolphins came close, we all began swimming alongside them. Suddenly there was a small splash: Alex, wearing a flotation device, had dived off the back of the boat.

She took to the water as if she had been a swimmer all her life. Removing the flotation device and tossing it back into the boat, she swam over and joined us with the dolphins. A little later, swimming with an assistant, she went snorkeling for twenty minutes. She was a natural.

What happened? Once we were able to clear the impact of that initial asteroid strike, the entire cloud of dust and debris associated with it dissipated and disappeared.

A Death by a Thousand Cuts

Sometimes the "event" is not a single occurrence on a given hour and day, but a series of experiences spread out over time.

Caitlyn was twenty-six years old when her car broke down one day on the freeway. After nearly an hour of waiting, the tow truck arrived. In a space of twenty minutes, the driver fixed her car and had it back on the road. Caitlyn paid the man and was safely on her way.

But while her car was fine, Caitlyn was not.

Within a few days, Caitlyn realized that the event had triggered a genuine phobia of being on that freeway. Soon she was afraid to drive on *any* freeways, then on city streets. Before long, she could barely make herself get in the car to drive anywhere at all, other than the very short distance to her neighborhood store.

Getting rides from friends helped, but not enough. One day, while a friend was driving her to work, she became nearly paralyzed with fear as they drove over a bridge—the same bridge she had gone over hundreds of times before without giving it a second thought.

By the time Caitlyn came to see us, she had become severely handicapped. Not being able to drive is tough anywhere; in southern California, the freeway capital of the world, it was positively crippling. She could barely get to work and back, and her social life had slowed to a rush-hour crawl.

After Caitlyn told us what was going on, we began looking into what precipitating events might have happened in her childhood.

We soon learned that Caitlyn grew up in a family of perfectionists. In her childhood home, a premium was placed on being orderly and spotless. Her parents were very exacting, and she received a lot of criticism. "You didn't make your bed properly! You left a mess behind! Look, you spilled some food!" Each one, taken by itself, was a minor thing and hardly traumatic. But piled up one on top of the other, day after day, year after year, they had the cumulative impact of an asteroid strike. Like the death by a thousand cuts, Caitlyn's sense of self gradually bled out until she became thoroughly imprinted with the message, *Can't you do anything right?*

Of course, she had long since managed to put these constant criticisms "behind her" and had grown up to become a healthy, fully capable adult. But then something happened. The day her car broke down on that freeway, her familiar, helpless feeling of *having messed up once again* triggered an entire backlog of childhood emotions, and that old message rose up within her like a dragon awakened from slumber.

It's important to realize that at no point did Caitlyn have the conscious thought, "Oh, look at this, I got myself stranded on the freeway—I guess my parents were right all along. I *can't* do anything right." That was the message, but it was so well established and deeply entrenched that, like the annoying refrigerator hum we learn to ignore, she was not even aware of it.

And even if she had been aware of it, she likely would have dismissed the thought as silly. That message would scarcely have seemed justified by the circumstances. Hey, her car broke down: it could happen to anyone, right?

But the fog of distress acts beyond the province of logical, conscious thought. Caitlyn *knew* she was a bright, resourceful, capable, grown woman. Alex *knew* that neither a glass of water nor a stroll in the surf would hurt her. Stefanie *knew* she was not a bad, selfish person.

But knowing these things was not enough to make the critical difference. Conscious, logical thought cannot disperse that cloud of debris.

Traumatic Resonance

Why, if Caitlyn had been able to function normally for all these years, did a chance freeway breakdown affect her so strongly? Most of us have had to change a flat tire or call a tow truck at least once in our lives, and we have done so without falling apart. So why was this event different for her?

Because of a phenomenon called *traumatic resonance*.

If you pluck the low E-string on a guitar, you'll see the high E-string vibrate along with it, thrumming as if it had been plucked by a phantom finger. This happens because the specific vibration rate of the high E (660 Hz) is an even multiple of the E two octaves lower (165 Hz). In other words, they are not identical, but they sound closely *similar*. The same thing happens if you hold a tuning fork next to a piano and strike the key for A above middle C: the tuning fork will vibrate, too.

This is called *resonance*, a word that literally means "sounds again." When the vibrations of two different phenomena have a similar shape or frequency, we say they "resonate with each other." Another term for this phenomenon is *sympathetic vibration*.

Musical notes are not the only things composed of vibrations: so are thoughts and feelings, events and circumstances—and the same principle applies. If you hear an idea or opinion that you are in *sympathy* with, you might say it *resonates* with you.

We often find that an early childhood experience will leave its mark and then be reinforced or reactivated by events later in life that resonate with the early event, much as the sound of a car backfiring can trigger the traumatic memories of combat.

This is what happened with Caitlyn. Because it resonated strongly with a deeply held belief that she had formed very early in life, her freeway breakdown plucked the strings of her early childhood experiences, setting them into sympathetic vibration—and like a sudden cold triggering a dormant infection, or a strong wind stoking a pile of long-standing embers into a fresh blaze, that negative belief reared its ugly head.

The same thing was true for Stefanie. That original event at the age of seven left her with a deep, inarticulate sense that she was *bad and selfish*. As a grown woman, the impact of her painful divorce resonated with that same message. The *I am bad and selfish* of her divorce was such a clear echo of the *I am bad and selfish* of her childhood event that Stefanie experienced it as an asteroid strike all over again.

The two sets of events may have had no rational connection. But that didn't matter: they had resonance.

Your Story

The first step in the Four-Step Process is to identify the nature of *your* personal fog of distress, and that starts with finding the asteroid strikes in your own past.

Let's start by just relaxing for a moment and letting your mind amble back through your earliest memories.

When we see a client for the first time, one of the first things we typically do is take his or her history. People often feel an urge to talk things out, and sometimes this can take up the entire first session. Early in our practice, we noticed that we could go through an entire appointment, hearing a good deal of personal history, without having gotten to anything critical that we could really put our finger on. Often we would find ourselves at the end of a session saying something like this:

"In the next few days, before our next visit, we'd like you to write down the three or four most significant events in your life that you can remember, from as early as you can recall."

We soon found that we could help new clients more effectively by cutting right to the chase and giving them that homework right at the outset.

So let's have you do that now.

Take a moment to think back and reflect on the earliest events you can remember. Big or small, major or trivial, it doesn't matter. What is the earliest experience you can recall?

You don't need to think too hard about this. Just fish for a moment in your pool of early memories, and pull up the first event that nibbles on the line.

Go ahead: put the book down for a moment, and see what memory comes to mind.

HAVE YOU DONE THAT? Good; now take another moment to do the same thing a second time, and recall another early memory from your childhood.

NOW, ONE LAST TIME, throw the line out and fish for a third childhood memory you can bring to mind.

AS YOU CONSIDER EACH of these three memories in turn, ask yourself, *Is this overall a more positive memory or a more negative memory?*

You might have brought up images of happy times, thawing by the fire after an afternoon of sledding, the smell of Grandma's cookies baking . . . but the chances are better than even that the first events you thought of were *not* so happy.

Why? Because there is a natural tendency to remember the more painful events of our lives. Our minds are wired to imprint in our memory stronger emotional experiences over milder ones, and negative or painful emotional events tend to imprint longer than positive ones. Because of this, it is likely that at least two of your three memories were of more unpleasant experiences.

To a degree, this tendency is healthy: it aims to provide for our survival. It's good to remember exactly where in the forest you found those nice berries and that delicious honey—but it's more important to remember where you narrowly escaped being eaten by that hungry tiger. It is often through a bad scare or painful encounter that we learn some of our earliest and most valuable lessons. Once you've touched a hot stove, "Don't touch that!" becomes more than mere words.

The fact that an event has stuck in your mind as a clear memory does not necessarily mean it has had a lasting impact. Often childhood experiences with difficult or uncomfortable aspects to them truly *are* innocent events that cause no long-term damage. Negative experiences are, to a considerable extent, how we learn. Sometimes a glass of water is just a glass of water.

However, as we've seen, sometimes certain negative events can continue to exert their grip on us long after it serves any useful purpose for them to do so. Those are the memories we're looking for here.

The Investigation

The three memories you pulled up in the previous exercise may include one or more of these key events we're looking for, but then again, they may not. Let's take a few moments now to investigate the situation more systematically.

Ask yourself:

What painful or unpleasant events or experiences do I remember from my childhood that had a strong or deep impact on me?

Quite often people will key in on these significant experiences right away. Often they will be events that they haven't given much thought to for years, as happened with Stefanie.

"Now that you mention it," we'll hear clients say, "yes, something peculiar did happen when I was little. I haven't thought about this for ages. . . ."

We often hear "It's probably nothing, but . . ."—and typically the event that follows that *but* turns out to be quite significant indeed.

Another comment people frequently make is "Well, I don't remember very much . . ."—and then, once they start exploring one memory, it leads to another, and then another, and they soon find that they actually remember *a lot*. It can be like finding a half-inch bit of thread sticking out at the end of your sweater sleeve. You give it an innocent little tug— and before you know it, the whole sleeve has come unraveled.

Here are some examples of common traumas and microtraumas that may help jog your memories or help you identify early events that have left their mark. As you read through this list, check off those that apply to you:

- ❏ I was very sick.
- ❏ A family member was sick.
- ❏ I was hospitalized.
- ❏ My parents divorced or separated.
- ❏ I lost a parent, grandparent, other family member, or someone else I was close to.
- ❏ My pet died.
- ❏ My parents left me with someone else (even if this was for a short time).
- ❏ I was left alone (in a supermarket, at my grandparents' house, and so on).
- ❏ I lost a friend (they moved away, went to another school, and so on).
- ❏ We moved.

- ❏ I was in a car accident.
- ❏ I was not chosen for a team.
- ❏ I was teased.
- ❏ I was criticized or scolded by someone I respected.
- ❏ There was a lack of contact or affection in my home.
- ❏ I suffered a major disappointment or letdown (experienced as betrayal, even if it was innocuous or with good reason).
- ❏ I was hit or punished.
- ❏ I remember my parents yelling or arguing.
- ❏ I had a frightening experience with a dog (or other animal).
- ❏ Someone I trusted or looked up to betrayed my trust.
- ❏ My dad or mom remarried and suddenly there was someone else (stepparent, stepsiblings) in my family.
- ❏ I was bullied.
- ❏ I felt different from my peers (in physical development, abilities, ethnicity, and the like).
- ❏ I went through physical changes (a growth spurt, puberty, developed a physical handicap, or other change).
- ❏ I was humiliated or ashamed.

As you scan through this list, there are probably at least two or three statements that jump out at you and may trigger memories of your own.

If any additional memories occur to you, in just a moment we're going to ask you to jot them down. You don't need to write a detailed description, just a few words to identify each one.

And by the way, once you've identified a few events in your past, we're not going to ask you to get down on your knees and muck around in them. The point is not to *re-experience* the feelings or emotions of the past event, but simply to *identify* the event so you know clearly what it is and can refer back to it quickly and easily.

Often the best way to do this is to come up with a short phrase, even a single word or two, that will serve as a reference to the event.

"Seventh birthday"

"Hurt in the playground"

"Grandma died"

"Moved away"

"Car accident"

"Fell out of the tree out back"

"Hospital in second grade"

For Stefanie, it was "My first quarter." For Caitlyn, it was "Being criticized." For Alex, it was "That wave."

As you identify these early memories, you'll want to write them down because you'll refer back to them later as you go through the steps of the Four-Step Process.

If you aren't sure yet whether a particular memory is really significant or not, don't worry: we'll explore that question further in a moment. For now, let's just go with whatever experiences you've come up with so far.

Go ahead, take a moment now to identify these early memories and write them down.

Adult Experiences Count, Too

Not all asteroid strikes take place when we are children. Sometimes painful events happen in our teenage or adult years that continue to exert a powerful impact on us long after we think we have gotten over them.

Identifying these more recent events is helpful for two reasons. First, traumatic events from your adult past may be significant sources of current issues in and of themselves. And second, they may serve as clues or pointers to much earlier events, like Stefanie's divorce.

As you scan through the following list, think about any painful experiences that may have occurred in your teenage or adult years, and jot those down briefly as well. Again, check off those that apply to you.

- ❏ I had an accident or bodily injury.
- ❏ I experienced a health crisis.
- ❏ I developed a chronic health problem.
- ❏ I went through a divorce.
- ❏ I went through a painful breakup or dysfunctional relationship.
- ❏ I experienced a bankruptcy, business failure, loss of investment, or other financial reversal.
- ❏ I experienced a theft or break-in.
- ❏ I lost my job.
- ❏ I lost my home.
- ❏ A family member died.
- ❏ I experienced the loss of eyesight, hearing, or other mental or physical function.
- ❏ I lost someone close to me (through death, miscarriage, abortion, estrangement, or other experience).

More Clues to the Past

If nothing has come to mind, or you feel you haven't yet hit on anything that is very significant, that's okay. Give this time. Often these memories take a little time and patience to bring up from the pool of the past—especially from the earliest years of our lives.

We have very little capacity to remember consciously our experiences before the age of three or four (for reasons we will explore in chapter 5). And even later, throughout childhood, the character of our memories can be quite different from our adult memories.

Here are some pointers that can help the process along.

Ask Others

Ask a relative or family member, someone who knew you from early childhood, if anything significant happened to you that you might not remember.

We had a client who had a terror of hospitals. It turned out, when he was three years old he was whisked to a hospital in an ambulance by himself, with no parent or other family member present. He did not come up with that bit of his own biography; he himself had absolutely no recollection of it. In fact, he had no idea it had happened. It was not until he was in conversation with his mother one day that she said, "Hey, do you remember when you were three . . . ?" and she told him what had occurred.

Remember the event that gave Alex her deathly fear of water? It was her father who told us about this event, not Alex herself. In fact, she did not even have a clear memory of that day or of what had happened as she and her dad walked out into the surf.

Just because you don't consciously remember an event doesn't mean it hasn't had—and doesn't *still* have—a powerful impact on you. If it's something that you don't remember yourself, but it's a story you've heard from someone who knew you when you were young, put that down, too.

Cumulative Trauma

Again, as with Caitlyn's childhood, sometimes it is not the impact of a single event but the cumulative effect of many events. Not an asteroid strike causing nuclear winter, but the gradual effects of an overall climate shift. The slights at school day after day, the repeated taunts, being embarrassed by a parent over and over for making simple mistakes—spilling the milk one day, buttoning your shirt wrong another day, and so forth.

We'll see more examples of this kind of cumulative traumatization in the stories in these pages. It's a very common scenario.

Vicarious Trauma

Sometimes we are deeply affected by events that we do not go through ourselves but that happen to people we are close to, or even people we hardly know. For example:

- My brother or sister was hurt.
- My dad lost his job.
- My friend's parents divorced.
- A neighbor's house was vandalized.
- A student in my school fell ill and died.

Events we experience vicariously can have a far more profound impact on us than we realize.

Weighing the Impact

Sometimes, at this point in the process, people say, "I've got at least a half-dozen events on my list. How do I know which events really count? How do I know which one has had the most impact?"

In chapter 3, we'll explore a fascinating method for confirming which events have had the most impact on us and, more important, which ones are still having the most impact today. But making this distinction is mostly a matter of gut sense, and it is surprisingly easy once you get into it. After all, nobody knows you better than you.

For starters, look at the first memory on your list.

Take a few deep breaths and reflect back on that event or experience for a moment. As you do, notice whether or not you feel any emotional charge, any twinge of feelings about the event. Don't try to analyze it or figure out what it means. For now, we're just trying to determine if the experience has had a lasting impact that still exerts a force in your life.

Again, just because you *remember* a painful event does not necessarily mean it has had a lasting negative impact. Many people have been teased (who hasn't?), have moved, have lost a friendship, or have been harshly criticized without it having had any long-term effect. If a memory is simply a piece of your biographical information, an event from the past that you recall without any strong feelings attached to it, it probably does not play a significant role in your life today.

But if you have a memory that is uncomfortable to think about even now, this could be a source of negative belief. And if you feel resistant to exploring it, that too could be a sign that there is something meaningful about the experience.

By the way, this is not a question of whether you consider yourself as having had an overall happy childhood, or an overall unhappy childhood. We've seen thousands of people who describe their childhoods in generally positive terms, but that doesn't mean there weren't still individual events and experiences that caused them lasting pain.

By the same token, we've seen thousands of people whose early histories seem like Dickensian novels, full of incredible difficulties and harsh circumstances, yet who emerged from these tough beginnings as relatively healthy, whole, and happy people.

Write It Down

You may wish to write out a description of the remembered experience in some detail to bring it more clearly to mind. Close your eyes and recall, as best you can, exactly what happened, and then open your eyes and write.

Or, you may prefer just to recall the general feeling of it, without getting into it in detail. That's fine, too. There is no wrong way to do this. Connect with that past event in whatever way feels easiest or most natural.

Speak It Out Loud

Saying it out loud can be helpful. When clients tell us their discoveries, it's often the fact that they're speaking them out loud, and not that it happens to be us they're telling, that lets them feel the impact those memories have.

You can do the same thing, even on your own. As you identify an event from your past that has had an impact, simply describe it out loud as if you were telling someone. Speaking this into a recorder can be helpful, too.

Look for Resonance

Sometimes you'll notice right away that an event from the past has clear echoes in the issues you are dealing with today.

A friend of ours broke his arm falling out of a tree when he was young. As an adult, he was extremely uncomfortable going to doctors' offices; in fact, the mere smell of antiseptic was enough to make his palms sweaty. He never knew why—until we had a conversation about it and he matter-of-factly pointed out that the first time he remembered setting foot in a doctor's office was when he had his broken arm set.

A client was terrified of a big dog in her neighbor's yard when she was six. She was never bitten, but the dog would bark like crazy whenever she went by. As an adult, she had a strong apprehension about going into unfamiliar places or situations.

You see the connection? That's *traumatic resonance*.

As you consider each memory on your list, ask yourself, *Is there a connection between the substance of that experience and whatever issues are going on in my life today?*

When in Doubt, Write It Down

Do your best to identify events that have had a strong negative impact on your life. You might not remember all the specifics, but if you experience discomfort merely when reading any of the statements on the preceding lists, you most likely either have forgotten the situation or have shut it out from your conscious awareness years ago. Consider that statement as if it applies to you.

If you don't see any obvious resonance, don't worry. Even if you don't find any correlation between an early memory and whatever issues are going on for you now, the sheer fact that you remember this experience, the fact that it came up for you in the course of your interview with yourself, suggests that it may be significant.

Write it down.

If you're curious about it, if it doesn't feel entirely resolved, or even if it simply sticks out in your mind for no apparent reason—write it down.

Your Inherent Code to Joy

If you now have a list of several early events but are not 100 percent sure which is *the* most significant one, don't worry: you've got plenty enough to work with.

This is the beauty of the Four-Step Process: it's extremely forgiving. In other words, you don't have to worry about whether you are "getting this right." Even if you have no more than just a little information to go on, the process will still go to work and start dissipating that fog of distress.

Why? Because human beings are designed to self-correct.

The human organism is built to self-calibrate through what science calls *homeostasis*, which simply means we have a strong tendency to return to equilibrium, no matter how out of balance we become. This is why our body temperature so consistently gravitates to 98.6° and the pH level of our blood normally stays very close to 7.35. The same thing is true of our emotional state. There is an emotional balance built into us that our organism strongly wants to maintain and to which it will return if given half a chance. Remove the blockages that life's more painful circumstances have put in its way, and it will. It is like a gravitational pull—an inherent *code to joy*.

To illustrate just how strongly this innate tendency wants to bring us back into emotional balance, and how readily the Four-Step Process facilitates this happening, here is one more story before going on to the next chapter.

David's Breakthrough

A few years ago a journalist named David came to interview us for a story. As we described our work, we asked him to think of something that was nagging at him, something we could perhaps help him clear up, by way of demonstration. He thought for a moment, then said, "Well, okay, I guess I've got something." And he told us about a lingering resentment he had concerning a previous marriage.

We took him through the steps of the Four-Step Process and then asked him how he felt. He shrugged. "Not much different, really. A little lighter, I guess, but nothing dramatic. But then, this thing wasn't nagging at me that badly before, anyway."

We continued with the interview and then parted ways.

Late the next day we got a call from David. His voice practically burst through the telephone with excitement. "You will not *believe* what happened!" he said, and he told us what had occurred earlier that day.

That morning (the morning *after* we had met), David was scheduled to drive to a nearby hotel for an interview with a local author. At the last minute, something had come up requiring his interview subject to return home, and the man had left a message at the hotel asking David if he would mind driving out to his home to conduct the interview there instead.

David's heart had leaped into his throat. Not from this area, he was driving a rental car that had no GPS and he didn't know his way around. His subject lived out in Rancho Santa Fe, a half hour away and at the end of a long route of twists and turns out in the country.

But that wasn't the worst of it. As it turned out, unknown or unfamiliar road directions happened to be David's psychological Achilles' heel.

"All my life," David explained to us, "I have had an absolute panic about road directions. If I have to drive somewhere I've never been before, alone, with no one to be my navigator, I get paralyzed with anxiety. It doesn't matter if I have a good map and great directions. The moment someone starts to explain how to get there, my mind shuts down. I don't hear it, can't retain it."

Worse yet, the person at the hotel had been able to give him only vague directions. David had set out for his interview with no clear map or directions, quite sure that he would be hopelessly lost within minutes.

"And get this," he said. "Not only did I *not* get lost, I never had a single moment of anxiety. I rolled down the window, enjoyed the scenery, and casually just *drove*, way out in the middle of nowhere. I never panicked, not even for a moment—and I found my way there with no problem whatsoever. I know this sounds nuts, but this has never happened to me before!"

Remember, we had not intended to treat David for this issue. In fact, we were not aware that he *had* this issue. He had not said a word to us about it. We thought we were treating him for one thing, and given that slight opening, David's innate sense of emotional homeostasis leaped at the opportunity to heal an entirely different problem—one we didn't even know existed.

That's how versatile the Four-Step Process is—and how powerful.

Where to Go from Here

At this point, you should have one or more memories singled out to focus on. In chapter 3, we'll return to this self-investigation and learn a fascinating technique for evaluating the impact these past events have had in your life. But first we need to look at the second piece of this picture.

Up until now, we've been focusing on the asteroid strike itself. Now it's time to turn our attention to that dust cloud of negative beliefs and see exactly what it looks like.

2

Seven Limiting Beliefs

Who you gonna believe, me or your own eyes?
—Chico Marx, in *Duck Soup*

WE WATCHED IN SHOCK and disbelief as the big man fell to his hands and knees and crawled. He kept crawling slowly for the next fifty feet or so, until we had reached the end of the little elevated corridor. At that point, he was able to get back up to his feet, albeit shakily, and walk with us normally.

We were at a conference with our friend Clay and had just passed from one wing of a conference center to another, our route taking us through an enclosed walkway suspended over a grassy area some twenty feet below. The windows along the passageway's walls provided a lovely view of the peaceful surroundings, but the windows were firmly shut. It was literally impossible to fall or tumble from the walkway, and even if one could, the greatest danger would have been a twenty-foot drop to the soft, rolling lawn beneath.

But none of that mattered to Clay, whose fear of heights was so profound that he had practically pressed his body against the carpeted walkway while we walked with him.

Seeing him so fervently glued to the floor was odd enough. What made it even odder was that we knew what Clay did for a living. A retired fighter pilot and decorated veteran, Clay was now a professional pilot for a major airline.

During the week, he flew 747s back and forth across the Atlantic.

We asked Clay how it was that he could fly massive planes filled with hundreds of passengers 30,000 feet over the ocean and experience no anxiety whatsoever, yet the prospect of walking across an enclosed walkway twenty feet above a grassy slope reduced him to a terrified puddle.

"The plane is my office," he said. "When I step into the cockpit, I know what to do. My training takes over, and I know I'm in control. I know it doesn't make any sense," he added. "But that's the best I can explain it."

At the controls of a 747, Clay could rely on his training and skills. Outside the cockpit, he was at the mercy of a different force. Making his way across that enclosed walkway, Clay told us, he *knew* logically that he was perfectly safe. His eyes *told* him he was safe. But neither his eyes nor his knowledge could change what he *believed*.

Clay grew up under the same roof with a terrifying father, a man who drank heavily, often flew into rages, and beat his son at the slightest provocation. The boy lived his young life literally on the edge, never knowing when in the next instant he might be pushed violently off. At the age of fourteen he ran away to strike out on his own. He never spoke to his father again.

As an adult, Clay grew to become one of the most generous, likeable, genuinely wonderful people we have ever met, and he carved out a very successful flying career. His highly developed skills served like a floodlight, chasing away the shadows of his childhood. But in circumstances where his skills did not apply, that old familiar darkness took hold again, crystallized around the core belief he had formed in his earliest days:

I am in danger.

The Threads That Run Our Lives

With advanced methods of brain imaging, and especially functional magnetic resonance imaging (fMRI), scientists in the past two decades have gained an astonishing ability to peer into the physical workings of the brain and watch these things unfold in real time.

Before the advent of real-time brain scans, scientists believed that the process of cell division that creates new brain cells, called *neurogenesis,* slowed early in life and stopped altogether by adolescence. Likewise, the process of *neuroplasticity,* the brain's ability to change the shape and structure of its pathways in response to our experiences, was until recently thought to be a phenomenon exclusive to infancy.

Not anymore. Dramatic findings of the past two decades show that neurogenesis and neuroplasticity continue throughout the human life span. No matter what your age, your brain is perfectly capable of creating entirely new neural pathways.

When an event happens, our perception of it occurs in the form of a distinct pattern of nerve firings through specific synapses (connections). In some cases, this involves not simply the firing of electrochemical impulses through existing networks, but the growth of new synapses and new neural networks. In other words, the brain can change its wiring in response to novel information. The more powerful and emotionally charged that information is, such as happens in traumatic experiences, the more rapid and significant the development of new neural connections will be. And the more this information is repeated, the more these new nerve pathways tend to form.

Picture what happens when it rains on a mountaintop. As the rain runs down the mountainside, rivulets forge pathways through the pebbles and pine needles scattered over the ground. Every time it rains, more water runs down the hill, carving that network of pathways a little deeper each time. Eventually these pathways become a stream, and then a river. If there is a powerful thunderstorm, the cascading torrents are far more likely to form deeper gulleys as they course down the mountain.

This is much like what happened with Clay's neural network in response to the painful experiences he had with his father. Every time he had a similar emotional and psychological response to the erratic and overbearing behavior, the yelling and beatings, a distinct pattern of nerve firings was amplified, a pattern that corresponded to the belief *I am in danger.*

This phenomenon has given rise to an expression in neuroscience: "Synapses that fire together, wire together."

And this is not just a saying; it is literally what happens. Through repetition, what started as a response to a singular event becomes progressively strengthened as our synapses grow new neural tissue, laying down an ever-thicker matrix of nerve fiber. Eventually that response pattern becomes a firmly embedded neural net that represents a fixed way of perceiving the world and events around us.

To use a different analogy: picture the way houseplants shift position and turn to grow in the direction of the sun. In the same way, our synaptic networks shift and grow in the direction of our most emotionally charged thoughts and experiences. This is how we form beliefs: we literally *grow* them, like a dynamic topiary of the mind.

The resulting beliefs are stronger than feelings, deeper than thoughts. Beliefs are patterns of thought so ingrained in our neural networks they have become automatic, like entrenched habits of thinking. They are the bedrock of our psychological architecture.

In the course of working with thousands of people in helping them to uncover their own self-limiting beliefs, we have found that most fall into one of seven patterns, which we have come to call the *seven common self-limiting beliefs:*

The Seven Self-Limiting Beliefs
1. I am not safe.
2. I am worthless.
3. I am powerless.

4. I am not lovable.
5. I cannot trust anyone.
6. I am bad.
7. I am alone.

In this chapter, we're going to examine each of these limiting beliefs in turn, to gain as full an understanding as possible of each one, what it looks like, and the kinds of experiences that can trigger it.

I Am Not Safe

Remember David, the journalist who was terrified of driving to unfamiliar locations? The next time we got together with David in person, we explored the matter a little further to see if we could help him pinpoint where this fear came from. We asked him if there were any events early in his life that might have caused any sort of trauma.

"Well," he said, "I don't know if this is relevant" (there it was again: that telltale *this is probably nothing, really*), "but something pretty weird happened when I was five."

Shortly after his fifth birthday, David traveled to Europe with his parents and older brother. They were in London at a theater, about to go inside for what would be David's first movie. While the parents stepped to the ticket booth to purchase their tickets, David and his brother milled around, looking at the movie posters behind their glass displays.

Suddenly an old woman appeared, bent with age, and took David by the hand. "Lost, are ye?" she crooned. "Come, come, we'll find yer parents." And she began leading David away down the street—*away* from the theater. Bewildered but unsure of what he should do, young David felt himself walking away with her.

Within moments, two London bobbies appeared. One gently led the old woman away while the other brought David back to his parents' side. The woman was well known to them, the second bobby explained to David's parents. She had lost her own child many years earlier, and this was not the first time she had tried to make up for it by "borrowing" someone else's.

The whole kidnap attempt took less than sixty seconds, from the moment the woman appeared until the bobby had reunited David safely with his parents.

"In fact," David said, "I barely have any recollection of the event itself. I dimly remember the old lady's voice, at least I *think* I do. But the only reason I even know what happened is from hearing my mother retell the story. If this had had some big traumatic impact, wouldn't my memory of it be more vivid?"

Not necessarily. Often very early events, even dramatic ones such as this, are very difficult to recall clearly. But even though he does not remember it consciously in any detail, the memory *is* still recorded vividly in the fabric of David's being—along with the belief that young David's brain formed at the time and that he has carried with him ever since:

I'm not safe.

When we emerge from the womb to be born into this world of new sights and sounds, dangers and opportunities, one of our first priorities is to learn how to keep ourselves safe. Self-preservation, the urge to protect our own safety and survival, is the strongest of all instinctual drives. This impulse starts on the most basic physiological level and, as we grow, it extends to our emotional lives and sense of identity. Eventually, as we become adults and, for many of us, have children of our own, that impulse of preservation extends to our families.

But no matter how vigilant we are, both for ourselves and for those we love, it's inevitable that this protective net will break down at some point. We have all experienced times, whether extended periods or mere moments, when we knew we were *not* safe, moments when our defenses were not enough, and we felt our own existence threatened.

Whether this threat to survival is literally true or only our perception makes no difference at all in terms of the impact the experience has on us. And in situations when that perceived threat serves as an asteroid strike on our emotional ecology, it can result in a persistent belief that keeps us in a permanent state of hypervigilance, unease, and anxiety for our safety, even when there is absolutely no rational threat in our surroundings.

Janice, a single woman in her late twenties, came to see us because she was having a difficult time sleeping. Not only was it hard to get to sleep, but once she was asleep, she was easily awakened again by the slightest sound. She often imagined noises and was beset by various irrational fears. She was so exhausted she was on the verge of a collapse.

In our first visit, we explored her history, but Janice could not think of any specific event that might have led her to feel this way. We gave her our "homework," asking her to reflect back on her childhood during the week and jot down the two or three earliest memories that occurred to her.

Sure enough, when she came back the following week for a second visit, she told us about an event she had meanwhile recalled.

One summer, when she was a child, her family had gone on a vacation, and when they returned, her parents were convinced that someone had broken into their house while they were away. No valuables were missing, and there was never any clear, conclusive proof that the break-in had in fact occurred. But the event left a deep impression on Janice that she described as *a sense of violation*.

It took working with the elements of the Four-Step Process for about a week until Janice began to feel sufficiently at peace that she could sleep through the night.

The thing that's remarkable to notice here is that not only did Janice herself *not* experience the precipitating event, but there was considerable doubt as to whether or not the event itself ever actually happened. Still, her parents believed that it had, and Janice's vicarious experience of her parents' sense of violation was enough to make a lasting impact.

It's also interesting that at first Janice was not able to put her finger on any experience from her past that might have triggered her irrational fear. The memory of her parents' break-in experience came only when she spent some time making a concerted effort to think back.

This is quite common, as we saw with the story of Brenda.

A woman in her sixties, Brenda came to see us because she had a fear of bridges. A healthy, capable, and fully self-sufficient person, Brenda nevertheless could not drive or walk over bridges and could ride in elevators only with extreme difficulty. Rationally, she knew the elevators and bridges were safe, but her rational sense could not even come close to overriding her deep sense of panic in these situations.

We began exploring her childhood and asked if there were any significant times in her early life when she did not feel safe. Like Janice, at first Brenda could not pinpoint anything specific. Finally, after she'd spent perhaps a half-hour talking about different events of her childhood, a stunned expression came over her face and she said, "Oh, yeah. . . ."

Brenda's mother died when she was nine; soon afterward, her father became abusive. She remembered one day when he had gotten very drunk. They got into an argument—and he started to choke her. She managed to scream loud enough so that a passing paperboy heard her and ran to get help from her neighbors, who came and stopped the man from seriously hurting her.

"If they hadn't come," she said, "I wouldn't be surprised if he would have killed me."

When she turned thirteen, Brenda ran away from home to get away from her dad. After a few months of living on her own, she called a priest, just to have someone to talk to. He promised to keep her confidence, so she told him where she was staying. But the priest had lied to her: he immediately told the police, who came and forcibly took her back to her father.

No wonder Brenda felt unsafe! And yet, incredibly, she had brushed these memories out of her conscious mind. It's not that she had literally forgotten them. She knew they had happened—but for years, she had simply avoided thinking about them. This is far more common than one might suspect.

As an adult, Brenda had learned how to take care of herself and keep herself safe—but emotionally the impact from those events was still in there, creating a wave of inescapable panic when faced with anything in her environment she could not control, even a little footbridge.

For some, this *I'm not safe* belief shows up in the form of very specific fears, such as David's anxiety about unknown locations, Janice's fear of nighttime noises, or Brenda's fear of bridges. For others, it exists as a general sense of anxiety, nervousness, or insecurity. It can lead us to feel hopeless, afraid to try new things, afraid to make any efforts to change our lives for the better.

Here are some of the forms this belief can take:

I can't protect myself.

I am in danger.

Everything around me is dangerous.

There is no place safe for me.

I'm vulnerable.

It's not okay to show my emotions.

I've been abandoned.

Take a moment to reflect on whatever issues are happening in your life today, and see if any of these statements resonate with you.

I Am Worthless

Some years ago, we gave a public presentation on the methods of the Four-Step Process. When it came time to do a demonstration of some of the bioelectric clearing techniques (we'll learn these in chapter 4), we asked for a volunteer from the audience. A woman came up from the third row and introduced herself: her name was Jeanne, and she was an attorney.

We asked Jeanne to choose an issue to work on but to keep it to herself. She didn't have to think: without blinking an eye she said, "I've got it." She did not say out loud what it was.

We demonstrated several elements of the Four-Step Process. Because we knew nothing about her past negative experiences or the particular self-limiting beliefs she was wrestling with presently, we obviously could not be at all specific in the *identify* step. We simply asked her to think about whatever it was she was dealing with and then went on with the rest of the process.

After the demonstration was over, Jeanne returned to her seat and we did not see her again—until she appeared at our office a year later, saying she wanted to tell us what had happened in the months since that event.

Even after she explained who she was, we almost did not recognize her.

She told us that she had grown up with a father who constantly criticized her, and (although she had never realized this before) this had created in her an unshakable sense that she was worthless and incapable. As an adult, she married a man who continued in a similar pattern, to the point where he was verbally abusive and eventually physically abusive as well.

"When you talked about the kinds of self-limiting beliefs we sometimes have," she told us, "you mentioned that one of those beliefs was *I'm not worthy*. That clicked for me. My husband had been treating me horribly—and because of my own feelings of worthlessness, I had been just *letting* him do it."

But all that had stopped the day Jeanne had been part of our demonstration.

"That day changed my life," she said. "After that, I stopped taking it. In fact, I filed for divorce. Today, he is out of my life. I've realized that

I'm worth something, and *nobody* is going to treat me like I'm not—not even myself."

Which brings us to the issue Jeanne had been wrestling with: her weight.

Years earlier, as a way of shielding herself from the abuse her husband was dishing out, she had started taking on some extra weight. Quite a bit of extra weight. In the year since we'd met her, Jeanne had dropped nearly *one hundred* pounds. Which was why we almost didn't recognize her at first.

In the months that followed, she went on to lose another fifty. Today Jeanne runs a business devoted to nutrition and personal health, through which she helps hundreds of women regain their own sense of self-worth.

Self-worth is a fragile thing. At birth, we have virtually no awareness of ourselves as autonomous individuals. Fully engaged in soaking up and learning from the world around us, we don't even realize that there *is* such a thing as "me." As our sense of identity emerges and develops, we begin establishing a healthy feel for our own worth as self-determining beings in the world. But in those early years, it doesn't take much to deal that sense a significant blow.

We all have the experience of falling short in our efforts. But sometimes the experience of not measuring up to expectations (ours or others'), or of being *told* that we are not measuring up, has the impact of an asteroid strike on our consciousness. The belief we form out of that bitter experience is that *we are inadequate; we are worthless; we are a failure.*

Failing is a normal part of life. In the course of learning to walk, one of our earliest achievements, we fall down repeatedly, and the same holds true for pretty much every other accomplishment in our lives. We learn by trying, failing, correcting, and trying again. But there is a world of difference between knowing that I failed at a specific task and concluding that *I am a failure.*

People with this belief may go through life with an undercurrent of anxiety that completely contradicts their outward sense of self-assurance, a deep sense that, despite their apparent talents, skills, and accomplishments, they are secretly empty and hollow, that their supposed gifts are all somehow fake. "I'm an imposter," they feel, "a fraud. If they really knew who I am, they'd fire me."

A minister by profession, Richard was a genuinely inspirational speaker. Funny, engaging, and uplifting, he exuded the self-confidence of someone who is completely comfortable in front of a group.

"If his congregation only knew the truth!" his wife told us the day they came to see us together. The truth was that Richard worried incessantly all through the week leading up to every sermon, and by Sunday morning he would be a wreck.

"He sounds fine and looks fine," his wife added, "and everyone loves the sermons. But inside, he's miserable."

If there were an Oscar for Best Performance by Clergy, Richard would have won it. Even worse than the anxiety was the gnawing sense that he was a fraud.

When Richard came to our offices, we helped him identify the self-limiting belief that was getting in his way. Once we began talking about his past and letting him reminisce on the events of his childhood, it did not take long.

One day, when Richard was just eight years old, a teacher called on him to stand up and give a brief report to the rest of the class about a chapter in a book they were all to have read over the week.

Richard rose, his stomach in knots, turned slowly to face the class, and froze. He was tongue-tied.

"To this day," he told us, "I have no idea why I couldn't describe that chapter. I'd read it, and enjoyed it. But all of a sudden, facing all those kids, I just went blank."

As Richard recalls it, the teacher was quite compassionate, and after it became clear that Richard was not going to stand and deliver, she gently told him he could sit down again and called on another student. But Richard clearly remembered the feeling as he looked around the room, heard the snickers, and saw the faces making fun of him. He was mortified.

He had not put it into words, but the feeling he had in that moment was vivid: "What an idiot. What a jerk. I know the material—but I can't even talk!"

This was the only time Richard could recall when he froze and was unable to speak. After that, he went out of his way to push himself to speak, every time he was called upon. He even rehearsed lines in his head beforehand and in time became quite eloquent. But even though he never let it show, that feeling of having been embarrassed in front of the whole class never went away. *I am a failure*, his internal voice kept telling him, even as he developed into an accomplished speaker.

Sitting with Richard as he told us his story, we took him through the Four-Step Process.

A week later his wife called us to tell us how dramatically he had changed. After clearing this negative belief and installing a positive belief in its place, she said, Richard had become a different person. He was giving his sermons as flawlessly as ever, only now his joy was genuine.

"You're the only ones I can really tell," she added. "Nobody else knew what he was going through. No one else saw the torment, week after week, for years on end. I just wanted to thank you and tell you that this isn't just an improvement—it's an utter *transformation*."

This *I am worthless* belief often stems from growing up in an environment of being criticized or evaluated negatively, as was the case with Jeanne, or from incidents where we were put on the spot and embarrassed, as was the case with Richard. Whatever the particulars of the event or original circumstances, we begin with a singular situation and then generalize that to become a blanket statement about ourselves, our abilities, or our value as a human being.

At its extreme, this conviction of one's own worthlessness can lead to self-destructive or hopeless thoughts, including suicide, the ultimate expression of a lack of self-worth. More commonly, it manifests as a nagging sense of inadequacy. People with the *I am worthless* belief often have difficulty asserting themselves in any situation, whether that means asking for a raise or asking for a date.

Another common expression of this belief is "I'm no good at . . ."— and you can fill in the blank with practically anything. *I'm no good at math. I'm no good at mechanical things. I'm not very good at social situations. I don't know how to talk to the opposite sex. I can't dance. I can't sing.*

The self-limiting variations are endless. In most cases they are not based on anything factual at all: most people who assert that "I'm no good at math" are in fact no worse in their basic mathematical capabilities than their peers, and the same goes for the rest of the common self-condemnation assertions.

Unfortunately, while this may often be so, it does not necessarily remain so. Like all self-limiting beliefs, the *I'm no good at . . .* belief can over time become a self-fulfilling prophecy. The person who is convinced he cannot carry a tune will not try, and the more he doesn't sing, the less chance he has of developing that ability. Keep telling yourself that you're no good in social situations, and in time it will become the truth.

The *I am a failure* version of this belief involves the fear of success as well as the fear of failure. These are two sides of the same coin. After all, if I believe I am a failure, then what would happen if I succeeded at something? Then I would be expected to succeed again in that area— and then it would be even more painful when I eventually failed, which I'd be certain to do, right? So better not to succeed in the first place: don't do anything that would make me stand out or get noticed.

The attitude is: Don't hold your head too far above the crowd. Don't stand out, don't excel, don't draw undue attention to yourself. Don't rock the boat.

Here are just some of the infinite variations on the theme of this belief:

I am not worthy (of success, happiness, and so forth).

I am a fraud.

I will never be successful.

I cannot succeed, no matter what.

I have to be perfect.

I am inadequate.

I am unimportant.

I am insignificant.

I am incompetent.

I am not good enough.

I am not smart enough.

I am not attractive enough.

I am no good at math (at sports, at parties, at fixing things, at cooking, at sex, and so forth).

I am useless.

I am a disappointment.

Take a moment and see if any of these statements resonate with you.

I Am Powerless

When Carmen came to see us, she was wrestling with a difficult and urgent issue. She had negotiated a divorce settlement, and it was now time to either sign the agreement or else go to court—but she couldn't do either one.

"I don't know what's wrong," she told us. "I just . . . I just can't make a decision. What if it's the wrong one?"

Carmen was so paralyzed with fear that she was now on the verge of completely losing the settlement she had so painstakingly worked out and being forced to go back to square one, which would have been a disaster.

As we helped her explore her history, she soon discovered what this paralyzing fear was and where it came from.

When she was a young girl, Carmen and her brother lived with their mother. Although the brother was a year younger than Carmen, he was bigger and stronger. Often, without provocation or warning, he would punch her or even beat her up. Struggling to keep the household afloat, her mother had a heavy work schedule and was seldom around to protect her.

Not surprisingly, Carmen formed a limiting belief that said, "I am not strong enough to take care of myself."

Fast-forward to present times. Despite a college education and the conscious awareness that she was a grown-up now and strong enough to take care of herself and fight for her rights, that voice from deep inside continued whispering its constant message:

I am powerless.

As a result, she could not muster the inner strength to see this divorce through to its conclusion.

We all seek to maintain a basic level of control over what happens in our lives. This is part of growing up, part of becoming an adult. When we feel powerful, we believe that we can accomplish *anything* we set our minds to, and the fact that we believe this galvanizes our minds and our bodies to help us do just that.

Unfortunately, the same is true of our self-limiting beliefs. To the extent that we come to believe we have no control over events, we tend to *give up* that control. When we believe we are powerless, we give away our power.

This belief is similar in a way to the belief that *I am worthless*. The difference is that people with the *I am powerless* belief do not see themselves as worthless—they just don't see themselves as having the ability to assert or exercise their worthiness in a way that will have any impact.

Almost as far back as he could remember, Michael had always been reserved and shy. In grade school, he was the last one chosen for the team, and he seldom raised his hand in class, even when he knew the answer to the teacher's question.

This pattern persisted even after Michael reached adulthood. He never asked for a raise at work, or applied for promotions, or in any way took initiative to be recognized, even though he consistently received good evaluations. Michael never had the experience of self confidence, of feeling deserving of praise, promotion, or success. He had resigned himself to a life of mediocrity.

No one was more amazed and delighted than Michael when Janet, a bright and lovely woman he met in his community, fell in love with him. They dated for several years and then married. Within a year, his delight turned to despair as he realized that their young marriage was starting to fail. They sought help and were referred to us.

"When we were first dating," Janet told us, "Michael was not only charming and funny, he was also confident, even decisive. But once we tied the knot, he started to change, and a whole different Michael emerged, one with no ambition and no sense of self. I hate to sound blunt or unfeeling, but the man I married has turned into a wimp!"

It was clear that she loved him, and that she wanted their marriage to work as much as he did. But she could feel herself losing her sense of respect for Michael and, horror of horrors, the love she had felt for him as well.

When Michael was eight years old, his parents moved from Arkansas to California. At school, Michael was teased because he "dressed funny" and spoke with a "funny accent." Of the various nicknames the other kids had for him, eventually the name "Okie" stuck. When Michael protested and told them he was from Arkansas, not Oklahoma, it persisted. Even after months had passed and he was no longer the new kid in school, he was still mocked and made the butt of jokes.

Unfortunately, Michael's parents had their hands full—way too full to pay much attention to Michael's complaints about teasing. The oldest brother, Tommie, was getting into serious trouble at school, including several acts of vandalism that got him suspended twice in the first six months they were there. And as bad luck would have it, Michael's youngest sibling, a sister named Lizzie, fell ill and was in and out of the hospital throughout that fall and winter. Although Michael didn't realize how serious it was at the time, many years later he learned that Lizzie had nearly died that winter, and that it was touch and go for weeks. On top of that, both parents also worked and had the added challenge of adjusting to their new jobs in California.

Within this series of minor and major disasters, Michael's dilemma completely fell off the family's radar screen. He knew his parents loved him, and they were never mean to him, or yelled at him, or treated him badly—they just didn't seem to *see* him.

"I remember sitting around the dinner table," he told us, "and I would ask my mom or dad to pass the potatoes, and nothing would happen. It was like I wasn't even there—like I was invisible."

At the age of eight, Michael had not yet formed the ability to step outside his own perspective and grasp how things looked and felt from his parents' point of view. He had no idea how serious Lizzie's illness was, no clear sense of how badly Tommie was acting out, and no concept at all of the adult pressures of adapting to a new job in a different state. And he had no one he could talk to about any of this, even if he had been able to articulate it. All he could do was come to his own conclusions, based on his experience.

Michael concluded that *he just didn't matter*—that he had no real ability to affect his circumstances or make a difference. That he was powerless. These beliefs were never verbalized or clearly thought out—

but they were *felt,* and those emotional impressions inscribed that negative belief onto his being.

No wonder he never volunteered in class. Why bother? Either he would be laughed at because he gave the wrong answer, or he would give the right answer and *still* be laughed at. And nobody would do anything about it. And he carried this belief into adulthood, deeply fearing that his superiors would ridicule him for asking for a raise or a promotion.

When he first met Janet, the excitement of a new relationship stirred up so much positive emotion that it was able to quell that old negative program—at least for a while. But once they were married, now Janet was *family,* and there was a deep-seated belief that said, "My family doesn't see me, I am invisible around them." Sure enough, he soon reverted to his habitual *I am powerless* mode of operation.

Both Michael and Janet were fascinated as we explained this to them, and they both immediately grasped what had happened. Janet, as it turned out, had some issues and negative beliefs of her own that had also fed the problem (no surprise there—these situations rarely involve self-limiting beliefs on only one side of the equation!), and we worked with both of them for several sessions over the next few weeks.

However, Michael's demeanor transformed in that very first session. When they stood up to leave that day, he seemed to have gained several inches in stature and a distinctly firmer handshake. Looking us right in the eye, he said, "Thanks for seeing me." The moment the words left his lips, he heard his own unintended double meaning and grinned. The look Janet gave him in that moment was worth the price of admission. It was a look of adoring love together with an expression that said, "Oh, *there* you are!"

Those of us who have this belief in our own powerlessness often become withdrawn and learn to avoid social situations. To the degree that we act this way, the people around us can pick up our subtle cues and start treating us the way we expect to be treated. People start ignoring your opinions and thoughts, treating you as if you don't exist. It's not that they don't like you; they just don't think about you. Like Michael, you start to become invisible.

Here are just a few of the many ways this belief can express itself:

I am not in control.

I am helpless.

I am weak.

I don't matter.

I am invisible.

I cannot stand up for myself.

I am trapped.

Take a moment and see if any of these statements resonate with you.

I Am Not Lovable

"We're worried about Heather. It's been *three weeks* now—is there any way you can fit her into your schedule right away?"

Heather's parents were at their wits' end. Twenty-three years old, Heather was an intelligent, ambitious college graduate with a bright future. One day, without any warning or prior signs of trouble, her boyfriend of four years called to tell her he didn't want to see her anymore and that he had been secretly seeing someone else for a few weeks already—and he broke up with her right then and there, over the telephone.

Heather did not simply get upset—she completely fell apart. Day after day, she called the young man's phone in a desperate effort to rehabilitate the relationship. After he stopped taking her calls, she became despondent. Her parents became so concerned by her deepening desperation that they brought Heather in to our office.

With Heather, the immediate cause of her distress seemed quite obvious. But was it? Of course, when you discover your boyfriend or girlfriend has been unfaithful, it's normal to be upset, hurt, and angry. But her response was extreme. She wasn't simply upset, hurt, or angry. She was utterly shattered. Why? Because the event *resonated* with something deeper, something that was already present in Heather beforehand. It wasn't simply the boyfriend's cheating that paralyzed Heather. The betrayal stirred up feelings surrounding a belief about herself that Heather had already formed many years earlier.

When we first spoke with Heather and her parents, none of them could imagine what traumatic events might have happened to have so shaken her belief in her own self-worth and lovability. By all their accounts, she had led a distinctly happy childhood. Both parents loved her very much and did not hesitate to express it.

However, as we talked about her early years, two interesting facts emerged. First, when Heather was very young both her parents worked, and her father especially worked an extremely brutal schedule. As a result, while she certainly felt loved by him, she rarely saw him.

And then there was the second biographical fact: when Heather was five years old, her grandfather died.

Heather had been utterly devoted to her granddad, had loved him like a second father. It might be more accurate to say she had loved him like a father, period—since she hardly ever saw her actual father. And when her grandfather passed away, the one person who consistently made Heather feel that there was someone always there who loved her suddenly vanished.

After one session, Heather realized that the phone call from her boyfriend had awakened a deep sense she had had all her life but had learned to bury. It wasn't just that she no longer felt loved; she felt she was *unlovable*. Her boyfriend's rejection had confirmed a deeply held belief that, for her, love would inevitably end in disappearance.

In the same way that *I am safe* gives us a secure foundation for growing and exploring our world, *I am loved* provides an emotional bedrock for our growth as people. Humans have an innate craving to be loved, first by our parents, and then by our friends and significant others. When this foundation is shaken, it can have a devastating impact, and this can show up in surprising ways.

When Ruby came to see us with her husband, Joe, they were both in their eighties and had been married for more than a half century. However, a few years before this, Ruby had learned that many years earlier, Joe had carried on an affair with another woman that had lasted the better part of a decade.

The affair had now been over for a long time; in fact, Ruby only learned about the affair after the woman had died. Joe had admitted the truth and apologized to her repeatedly. He could not explain why he had done what he did, except to say he always loved Ruby and never intended to divorce or leave her.

As much as she wanted to, Ruby could not find her way to forgive and let go. She experienced bouts of anger and viciousness that, while they never got physical, nevertheless were frightening to Joe, who had become weak and unable to care for himself and physically depended on Ruby. He was beginning to genuinely fear for his safety.

"I want to let go," Ruby told us, "but I can't. It's almost like I am possessed. Anything that even vaguely reminds me of Joe's betrayal—even the mention of harmless words like *beauty, attraction,* or *secret*—will set me off."

After a year of watching her struggle unsuccessfully to let go and forgive her husband, Ruby's children encouraged her to come to our office.

Outwardly, Ruby was angry—but underneath that fury there lay a very different emotional conflict.

Ruby grew up with a mother who was harsh and critical, frequently disapproving of Ruby's choices in clothes, in friends, in anything and everything she did. She could not recall even once being praised for making a good decision. This had resulted in a deep belief that she was not lovable.

One of Ruby's strongest memories was of something that happened with her father when she was in eighth grade. A boy from her class walked her home from school one day—and when she got home, her father exploded at her.

"Boys only want one thing!" he said, and he told her she was never to walk home with that boy or any other boy.

For Ruby, this only reinforced her belief that she was not lovable: not only did her mother dislike every choice she made, but now her father had made it clear that no boy would ever love her for who she was.

As an adult, Ruby had gotten past that belief and had lived with Joe happily for decades. But when she learned of his past affair, it triggered that old, smoldering belief. It had never really gone away, only lain in waiting for the right evidence to come along and confirm its toxic message.

The emotional logic went something like this: *The fact that Joe was cheating on me behind my back confirms that I am not lovable, and never was. For a while there, I thought I was, but I was wrong—and if he persists in saying he loves me now, then he must be lying.*

The *I am not lovable* belief most often goes back to our parents or primary caretakers. It can stem from having had the sense that one or both parents loved one sibling more than the other. It may be that one or both parents was particularly cold, aloof, or undemonstrative, or simply not available.

Such situations and experiences may have nothing to do with the reality of the parents' love for the child. Even if your parents were wonderful, loving, encouraging, and supportive, there may easily have been incidents when you *perceived* as them withdrawing or withholding their love and support for you. They may have been burdened by a heavy work schedule or distracted by a health issue. Sometimes the most innocent circumstances can be misperceived by a child as abandonment—as we learned from Jack's story.

"I've pushed away every woman I've ever gotten close to," Jack told us in his first visit, "and if I can't figure out how to change, I'm about to lose my relationship with Greta—and she's the best thing that's ever happened to me."

Jack seemed completely calm and self-assured on the outside but, as we soon learned, inside he was a seething mass of anxiety.

As much as he loved Greta, and as much as she loved him, he felt she was not attentive enough. The constant demands he put on her to demonstrate her affection for him was starting to drive her crazy.

"I know it's extreme," he said, "and I know I'm obsessive about it. It's like I need her to be always telling me and showing me she cares about me. I know I'm just pushing her away, but I don't know how to stop."

As Jack described his childhood, a fascinating detail emerged.

When Jack was six, his mother had been hospitalized for several months. This was in the fall and happened to coincide with Jack's going to first grade, his first time in school. Although he had no conscious memory of this event, his teacher reported to his father that he was badly teased on his first day and that she had found him crying in the schoolyard.

All in all, Jack had very fond memories of his childhood and reported that it had been a generally happy home environment. But for that brief time, at a juncture in his young life when he sorely needed his mother's love, she wasn't there—and his young brain interpreted that experience as having somehow been his fault.

Although Jack never put it in these words, the emotional essence of the fog of distress that clouded his life was clear: *I am not lovable.*

In a later session, Jack recalled another memory that shed even more light on his situation.

One day, during the summer before first grade, Jack and his dad had secretly agreed to slip out of the house that Saturday to go buy his mother a birthday present, as her birthday was coming up that August. When that Saturday arrived, his dad absent-mindedly left the house alone.

Jack heard the car pulling out of the driveway and ran to the front door, screaming, "Wait! Wait!"—but his dad didn't hear him and drove off, not realizing his son was calling after him.

"I distinctly remember him driving off," Jack told us, "and me bursting into tears. My mom wanted to know what was wrong—but I couldn't tell her, because it was about getting a present for *her*."

Jack said it was one of his strongest early childhood memories. And this event occurred just weeks before his mother went into the hospital, depriving Jack of the love he needed as he "left home" for the first time to brave first grade.

As an adult, Jack could not shake the feeling that he was unloved and unlovable—and no matter how much validation and affection he got from the woman he was with, it was never enough to gainsay that deep belief.

With the help of the Four-Step Process, Heather, Ruby, and Jack were all able to surmount their difficulties.

Heather transformed her belief in herself as a lovable, capable person who was deserving of a truly healthy and loving relationship. When Heather's boyfriend (now ex-) eventually called to apologize and make up, Heather remained resolute and declined to get back together. She realized that he was not ready for the kind of relationship she wanted. She was able to set a clear boundary and move on with her life in a healthy way, feeling strong, competent, and confident about herself and her future.

For Ruby, it took longer, but the same thing happened. After nearly a month of gradual improvement, she reached the point where she could say the word *affair* herself without getting angry or crying.

For Jack, things were a little tougher. By the time he came to see us, Greta had just about had all she could take of his demanding pattern, and he was not able to salvage that relationship. However, once he was out from under that oppressive sense of his own unlovability, he was eventually able to enter a new relationship in a far healthier, more relaxed way, and he and his new girlfriend have been quite happy together.

The key point is that Heather *knew* she was pining beyond the point of reason; Ruby *knew* that she should forgive Joe and move on; Jack *knew* he was suffocating Greta with his incessant demands. But simply knowing these things was not enough to change them.

Variations of this belief include:

I don't deserve love.

I have no identity.

I do not deserve to have a loving relationship.

I should expect to be betrayed.

Take a moment and see if any of these statements resonate with you.

I Cannot Trust Anyone

"I don't see what I can really do to change this," said Tom. "I'm under a lot of stress at work." He and his wife Claire were in our office because they were at an impasse in their marriage. Claire felt he had grown distant; he felt she was not understanding enough about the stress he was under.

The tension was visible the moment they entered the office. It was clear that they cared for each other, but Tom's body language was guarded, and there was a sense that his warmth was forced and artificial.

They got right to the point. Claire wanted to have children, and Tom was not sure they were ready for that step. As a consequence, Claire did not want to use birth control—and this had made Tom leery about sexual intimacy. Even beyond the issue of sex per se, Claire felt he was withholding affection and attention, that he was withdrawing from her in general—and she was starting to feel resentful.

"I don't know what to say," Tom countered. "When I get home at the end of the day, I feel tense and wiped out. I'm trying my best to relax, but it's got me stressed out."

We began exploring both their childhoods, and within minutes the conversation gravitated specifically to Tom's history. He explained that he grew up in an emotionally cold environment, with a father who was especially aloof. When he was quite young, his parents divorced and his father moved away.

In a sense, Tom was traumatized by this separation, and his feeling of being abandoned by his father imprinted on him a fear of getting close. As an adult, he feared intimacy because he was afraid that he would lose it. After all, he had lost his father.

The truth was, his issues had nothing to do with stress at work; they stemmed from his fear of getting close to those he loved. His logical mind was using their differing views over whether to have more children as the reason for the growing distance between them—but it had nothing to do with children, and nothing to do with sex. What it had to do with was the fact that Tom was afraid that if he got close to Claire, he would lose her.

Tom's belief was "The people I love will leave." Ironically, he was well on his way to creating that very outcome. As so often happens, Tom's self-limiting belief was becoming a self-fulfilling prophecy.

Fortunately, Tom and Claire genuinely cared for each other and wanted to work this out. And with the help of the Four-Step Process, they did. Once Tom's anxiety and fear of intimacy lifted, the two were able to reestablish their strong connection.

As we are first growing and learning our way through life, trust is the glue that holds our world together. We learn to walk, talk, and interact with our environment and with other people within a framework that depends on trust. If we could not trust our senses, our own judgment, our environment, and the people around us, then we would have no solid foundation to build upon, and life would be completely unpredictable and terrifying.

It's no surprise, then, that when our sense of trust is violated or shaken, it can threaten the basis of our very existence—or feel like it does.

People with the belief *I cannot trust anyone* often feel they are always on guard, suspicious, or ill at ease. Because of the sense that they cannot trust anyone, it's very difficult for them to feel comfortable handing over the controls to others. They may be backseat drivers, micromanagers, or control freaks who drive those around them nuts. Or, they may have an equally hard time trusting themselves, and as a consequence, never let themselves fully participate in the fun unfolding around them. They may feel anxious about anything unpredictable or spontaneous, or seem not quite present in their own bodies, keeping themselves at a remove, like Tom.

There are two typical sources for this belief. First, experience with the key authority figures in our early lives, especially our parents. And second, the small, incremental disappointments that can happen in life. For those who have a more solid, healthier foundation, these disappointments slide off and do no lasting damage. For others who are more vulnerable, they can stick and create an ongoing problem, adding to the neural network that says, *I cannot trust.*

The betrayal doesn't have to be big. Of course, huge and obviously traumatic betrayals—being molested at the hands of a parent or trusted relative, a friend who spreads lies about you to gain status among schoolmates—clearly have an enormous impact. But even small disappointments and *perceived* betrayals can create a lingering sense of violated trust. The missed recital, ball game, or birthday party, the forgotten Christmas present.

Screenwriter Nora Ephron captures this beautifully in the film *My Blue Heaven*, in a scene where gangster-turned-federal-witness Vinnie Antonelli (played by Steve Martin) talks about what it's like for a kid to experience disappointment.

I know how it feels to be disappointed. When I was seven years old—no! eight—all I wanted for Christmas was a new, red bicycle. My favorite uncle, Uncle Alfresco, swore to me that he would buy me that bicycle. I counted the days till Christmas. Five o'clock, Christmas morning: I run downstairs and look under the tree. What do I find? Uncle Alfresco: dead. On the floor. Shot through the back of the head. Plus: *no bicycle.* It was a disappointing Christmas on many levels.

In reality, there may have been very good reasons behind what we perceived as the betrayal or abandonment. Dad may have been unable to get to our recital or ball game because the car broke down, or because he was working hard to provide for the family and had to stay late at the office. Mom may have found they just didn't have the money to buy the promised toy. Hey, Uncle Alfresco *couldn't* get Vinnie the bike: he'd been shot in the head.

But whatever the external reality or mitigating circumstances, our own perception is that someone we trusted has let us down—and that has set up a protective interference pattern in our belief system that says the world is not a place to be trusted.

This is similar in some ways to the belief, *I am not safe*. The main difference between these two is that the issue of *safety* involves more one's sense of physical and emotional security, while *trust* has more to do with issues around our sense of connection with human beings, both others and ourselves. Safety, in other words, pertains to our sense of the world around us, while trust pertains more to our sense of the people of the world—in technical terms, *external locus of control* versus *internal locus of control*.

Here are a few variations of this belief; take a moment and see if any of these resonate with you:

I can't believe what anyone tells me.

I don't trust anyone in authority.

I am not a trusting person.

I am not a trustworthy person.

I can't be trusted.

I can't trust myself.

I never make good choices

I'm bad luck.

I can't trust my judgment.

I Am Bad

Claudia's life was a puzzle. An extremely bright, talented person with a keen command of language and razor sense of humor, she had established quite a reputation as a web designer. Unfortunately, she couldn't seem to keep her best clients long enough to build profitable, long-term professional relationships.

"I don't know why I do it," she told us. "I don't even know *how* I do it! Apparently, I am a black belt master martial artist when it comes to self-sabotage."

She told us about her last three big clients and how, despite the fact that she got along fabulously well with them and they were all very happy with her work, she had somehow managed to alienate them or lose their trust to the point where, one by one, they had all dropped her and sought out other designers.

"Honestly, I'm good at what I do," she said. "And I could be making a very decent living at it. If I would just stop getting in my own way."

When we asked Claudia about her childhood, we got an earful.

Claudia and her younger sister grew up with their divorced mother and saw their father (who lived some distance away) only quite rarely. We soon understood how it was that Claudia had developed such a sharp wit and gift with language: she had grown up sparring with a mother who was intensely critical and quite harsh, even brutal, in the way she expressed it. Claudia had learned early on how to think on her feet.

However, no matter how good she had become at verbally deflecting them, the criticisms still stung. Jean, as Claudia called her (she could not bring herself to call the woman "my mother," even after all these years), routinely told Claudia she was a slut, a bad influence on her little sister, a wise-ass, self-centered, and lazy.

The truly whopping, dinosaur-killing asteroid came when Claudia was fourteen.

"One day," she told us, "I came home from school, and the apartment was empty. I mean, *empty.* Jean wasn't there, and neither was my sister Chloe. But that's not all. All our stuff was gone. Even the furniture."

While Claudia had been at school, her mother had literally *moved out,* taking Chloe with her.

Fortunately Claudia had a relative who lived nearby and was able to move in with her for a few weeks while they managed to track Jean down.

"She could run," Claudia quipped to us, "but she couldn't hide. I moved back in with her—but only until the day I turned sixteen. I've been out of there ever since."

It was no mystery why Claudia kept losing clients. Logically, she knew she was a good designer and a valuable, reliable resource to her clients. But deep inside, she had bought hook, line, and sinker into the charge that she was a bad person, lazy, slothful, selfish, and of no use to anyone. There was a part of Claudia that kept expecting her clients to pull up and move away suddenly—and when they didn't, she unconsciously sabotaged the relationship until they did.

There's hardly a child alive who hasn't been told that he or she has been "bad" by someone he or she trusts and respects. For a young child, still struggling to carve a sense of identity out of the welter of everyday experiences, simply being told "No!" or "Don't do that!" can be received as the message, *You are wrong! You are bad!* That's normal; it happens to all of us. For some, though, the accusation sticks.

Like Hester Prynne's scarlet letter, the person with this self-limiting belief wears a badge of condemnation that colors every experience she has.

The desire for our parents' and others' approval is innate in every one of us. Children naturally want to please their parents, and virtually every parent, at least at times, uses this vulnerability as a way to control the child's behavior. To an extent, this is normal and productive, both in keeping the child safe from harm and in helping her learn to make crucial distinctions in life. There is a tendency in some families, though, to overdo this, taking it past the point of instruction and into the realm of condemnation.

For example, there is a difference between embarrassment and shame. *Embarrassment* is about a specific action of ours that has brought us unwanted attention. *Shame* is unwanted attention brought to us for *who we are as a person*, not just for something we've done.

The child spills a glass of milk at the table and we say, "What's the matter with you?! How many times have I told you to be careful?" These are questions, of course, that have no answers, and the child is left with no way to respond—that is, unless we provide one.

In that same scenario, imagine the parent comes out with the same scolding, but then says, "Okay . . . look, go get some paper towels from the kitchen and just wipe it up, and it'll be okay."

The scolding still hurts, but now it's more embarrassment than genuine shame, and now the child has some capacity to atone, to redress the error through positive action. In other words, he is given a pathway to separate the clumsy deed from himself: he may have *done* something wrong, but that doesn't mean he *is* wrong.

Young children are especially prone to drawing this kind of self-indicting conclusion. As parents, one way to ensure that we don't contribute to this belief in our kids is to take care not to level accusations that broadly generalize. Statements that start out "Why do you always . . . ," or "Every time you . . . ," or "Why can't you ever . . ." create blanket statements of condemnation that are nearly impossible to defend against.

This unfortunate power to condemn is not exclusive to parents. In any relationship where one person trusts or cares about the opinions of the other, this dynamic can hold sway. Those same sweeping statements can just as easily be aimed from teacher to student, older sibling to younger, or spouse to spouse.

Guilt seeks punishment, and those with this self-limiting belief tend—typically without consciously realizing it—to do things that are not good for them or that are contrary to their intended goals and consciously held beliefs. In other words, as Claudia so accurately put it, to become *self-sabotaging*.

The story of Stefanie, the successful executive whom we met in the introduction and again in chapter 1, is a good example of this belief. When her parents scolded her for taking a quarter from her aunt, without consciously realizing it or putting it into words, the seven-year-old Stefanie had formed a belief about herself that went something like this:

I am shameful and bad.

As an adult, that lingering fog of self-recrimination had expressed itself this way:

I am not deserving nor capable of having success.

And sure enough, she had made choices and taken actions that, over time, aligned perfectly with that belief.

Here are just a few of the many variations of this belief:

I am wrong.

I am no good.

I am selfish and think only of myself.

I am guilty.

I should be ashamed of myself

There is something wrong with me.

I have disappointed myself, let myself down.

I'm terrible.

I'm shameful.

I'm sinful.

I cause misfortune.

I deserve only bad things.

I should have known better.

I Am Alone

One day a man in his forties showed up in our office and asked for an appointment. He did not want to fill out any intake forms, and he gave his name only as "Gabe X." He insisted on paying for the appointment in cash.

Gabe made a striking impression. Tanned and obviously quite fit, he moved like an Olympic athlete. He spoke with precision but in a near monotone, and his face betrayed a nearly total lack of expression. The clinical term is that he was *without affect:* more like a robot than a man.

Right away, he told us he'd been to see a number of therapists and (like Stefanie) had done quite a bit of reading on mood issues. Nothing had helped.

Gabe's life story was shocking. He never knew his father; his mother was a drug addict and abandoned him early on. He grew up with a distant relative who dealt drugs and was part of a gang. There were always guns lying around the house. One day, when Gabe was nine, he picked up a gun out of curiosity and it accidentally went off, killing another kid who happened to be there.

As an adult, Gabe had landed in the military in Special Forces and had shipped off to the hottest war zones, where he had served the country for some years as a sniper. Now he was retired from the service, trying to carve out a career in business and a life of sanity for himself.

And then he told us the problem he was wresting with.

"I feel like I have no soul," he said.

Gabe's problem went beyond common clinical terms such as *depression, anxiety,* or *post-traumatic stress*. The phrase *existential despair* perhaps comes closest. In the simplest terms, Gabe felt *cut off from life*.

To look at Gabe's dilemma from a slightly different angle, consider the story of Nathan.

Nathan came to us because his marriage of fifty years was in trouble. He loved his wife, Judith, but was too depressed to relate to her. She was quite outgoing and social, while he was more introverted, and he was irritated at her efforts to pull him out into her social scenes. For this and many other little things, he'd get angry at her, yell at her, and then feel terrible afterward.

Before even going to Nathan's history, we began talking about his present life. A retired engineer, he no longer needed to work. What did he do with his time?

"I don't know," he said with a sigh. "I've got a few hobbies and things I do. I guess you'd say, things I distract myself with. Honestly, I'm not really sure what to do with my life." He seemed a bit depressed and moody.

Once we started talking about his history, we found out why.

Twenty years earlier, Nathan had been out on an errand with his teenage daughter, Janie, who had recently gotten her driver's license. Janie was behind the wheel. As they passed through a quiet intersection just blocks from their home, a drunk driver careened through the light and rammed into their car broadside at sixty miles per hour. Janie's rib cage was crushed and she couldn't breathe, but they were both trapped so tightly in the wreckage that neither of them could move. Waiting helplessly for assistance to arrive, Nathan could do nothing but sit and watch his daughter slowly asphyxiate to death.

Was it any wonder he was depressed?

But here's the thing: as horrible and tragic as the loss of his daughter was, that wasn't what was eating Nathan up. Yes, her death was incredibly painful, but over the years, Nathan and Judith had both gradually come to terms with their loss. That wasn't what had such a stranglehold over his life. It was the lingering experience of futility—that he had been unable to do anything to stop the tragedy from unfolding.

She had died, while he sat there and did nothing.

Of course, there was absolutely nothing he could have done otherwise: he was held physically immobile by the same wreck that held his daughter. But that was exactly what had left such a terrible wound. It was not so much that he blamed himself as a pervading sense of abandonment and futility. How could life be so unfair? If such a thing could happen, what was the point of anything?

What had made this so difficult to see was that he had, as much as one can, "gotten over" the tragedy. It was now years behind them. And Nathan was not suicidal or walking around grief-stricken. There were no overt, dramatic symptoms. Just a dark, dense fog over his life. He was simply living his life in a state of disconnection.

When he would get angry at Judith, which was happening frequently, it was not Judith he was really angry at. He was simply turning his hostility outward in her direction.

Who he was really angry at was God.

We've seen so many people who have lost someone close to them, especially in devastating circumstances such as terrible accidents, violent crimes, or lingering illnesses, who have come out of the situation angry at God, even if they don't know it. Often people will deny this consciously, saying, "No, I believe in God, God works in mysterious ways, God must have a bigger plan," and so forth—but that can be the logical self talking. Meanwhile, the emotional self is profoundly cut off, so that we have a huge hole in us and don't even realize it.

We see this especially with the death of children, which seems so profoundly unjust. But we also see it in cases where a child has lost a parent early on, or a grandparent, or someone else he or she cared about.

We often see this in the grieving process: "Why would God let this happen?" is a very common question that comes up in grief support groups. Why would God allow a child to suffer? Why take a teenager in a car crash? In an event such as the terrorist attacks of September 11, 2001, or cataclysmic natural disasters such as the 2004 tsunami that killed nearly a quarter-million people, the 2010 earthquake that devastated Haiti, or the earthquake, tsunami, and nuclear meltdown that hit Japan in 2011, the experience of trauma and resulting sense of futility and loss of faith can be profoundly widespread.

In many cases, this anger is directed not at God but at oneself.

Another client, Deborah, had a son who died in a car crash in which he had been drinking. She was angry at herself because she felt she should have somehow done something to stop him from drinking and driving—even though she was not there at the time, and thus there was nothing she *could* have done.

It is not only situations involving tragic death that can evoke this angry-at-self sense. People often get angry at themselves for a breakup or divorce and feel guilty over its effect on their children or over problems their children have as adults. Severe financial loss or profound career setback, theft, a bitter divorce between one's parents . . . there are many circumstances when the turn of events can seem so profoundly unfair that our sense of justice in the world feels broken beyond repair.

This is also not exclusively about God. It is about our sense of connection, and about the loss of that sense.

Even people who subscribe to no specific faith or spiritual belief typically live with *some* sense of connection to a larger reality. Many people who do not necessarily claim to believe in God nevertheless have a sense of spirit, that there is a larger intelligence or order to the universe. To some, this is most strongly felt as a connection to nature, to the mountains and trees, sunset and foliage. Some feel this larger spiritual sense most strongly in their immersion in music or another art. Some feel it most clearly as a sense of connection to the larger human family.

At its simplest, it is our sense of connection to life itself.

When we feel that connection, then we are never truly alone. Conversely, when we do not feel that sense of connection—to God, to nature, to the larger family of humanity, to life itself—then when we are alone, we are *alone*. "The eternal silence of these infinite spaces terrifies me," wrote the seventeenth-century scientist Blaise Pascal—whose mother died when young Blaise was just three.

When people have no sense of connection outside themselves, it not only changes their outlook on life, it also changes their health. Their sense of hope diminishes and with it a healthy immune system function. The body can respond by a gradual cessation of that mysterious force that every medical professional knows as "the will to live."

Gabe's progress was remarkable. In the very first session, after we took him through the simple clearing steps we'll look at later in this book, his demeanor changed dramatically. The best way we can describe it is this: it was as if he had walked into the office in a black-and-white film—and had filled out in color by the time he left.

By his third session, he was genuinely smiling, even laughing.

For Nathan, it took some time to uncover his self-limiting belief and work through this process. It did not happen in a single session, but in a series of sessions over some months. But it worked. In time, that fog of hopelessness, alienation, and anger lifted to the point where his connection with his wife Judith reawakened. Since that time, he has become more engaged and directed in his activities, and the couple's relationship has improved enormously.

Not long ago they went on a cruise together. We received a letter from him, postmarked from Italy: "We haven't fought once! I have to tell you, it's so nice to be able to be with my wife and not feel that old familiar hostility."

Here are some examples of how this self-limiting belief can express itself:

I am alone.

Life is empty.

There is no point in going on.

There is no point in anything.

I am disconnected from the world.

I am disconnected from God.

I am angry at God.

I am angry at myself.

Your Own Personal Belief Assessment

As you've read through this chapter, you have probably felt one or more of these beliefs resonating with you. Your goal now is to identify which holds the greatest sway in your life.

To help you zero in on this, here are seven sets of statements that exemplify these seven beliefs. As you read through each set, check those statements that feel like they fit for you and your everyday experiences, even if only somewhat so.

As you do this, also refer back to the significant experiences from the past that you identified in chapter 1, and consider those in relation to these beliefs. Do you see any correlations?

"I Am Not Safe."

❏ I cannot shake the sense that I am in danger of imminent harm, fatal illness, or other threat to my being.

❏ I often avoid or am uncomfortable in social situations where there are a lot of people I don't know well.

❏ I worry constantly about my health and always seem to have something going on that's wrong with me.

❏ My family says I am overprotective, but I can't seem to stop hovering over them and worrying about them.

❏ I tend to feel anxious in enclosed spaces/open spaces/heights.

❏ It's difficult for me to show my emotions, even with those I love.

❏ When conflicts happen, I do everything I can to avoid them rather than face them.

❏ I often feel paralyzed when making important decisions.

"I Am Worthless."

❑ I don't allow myself to pursue a certain skill, career, sport, hobby, or other activity, even though I know I'm capable of it and would enjoy doing it.

❑ I am uncomfortable speaking in front of groups.

❑ I feel I am a fake, I don't deserve the respect I have from others, or I am not as good or worthy as I might appear to be.

❑ I often don't ask for what I believe is a fair or reasonable request out of fear that I'll be rejected.

❑ I have a hard time sticking up for myself when people criticize me or treat me poorly.

❑ I seem to often get into relationships in which the other person doesn't treat me well or with respect.

❑ Others have told me I don't pay enough attention to the way I look or dress.

❑ Whenever I do something new, I have a hard time shaking the expectation that I will fail.

❑ In my relationships/in my career, I have the feeling that I have "settled."

❑ I often feel like the people I spend time with are smarter, funnier, more talented, and so forth than I am.

❑ I feel like a burden to my family/the people around me.

❑ I often worry about disappointing others.

"I Am Powerless."

❑ In a group, even a small one, I often feel invisible.

❑ I sometimes feel like a stranger, even among people who know me.

❑ I sometimes feel trapped in my job/in my relationship/in my career/in my life.

❏ I find myself wondering, if I suddenly disappeared, would anyone really notice or care?

❏ I keep getting passed over for recognition, promotions, or other acknowledgment.

❏ My life feels like a merry-go-round or carnival ride that I have no control over.

❏ I have a problem with alcohol/cigarettes/overeating/other addictive substances or compulsive behaviors, and even though I realize these behaviors are harming me, I don't feel I can stop.

❏ I worry constantly about the state of the world and feel that nothing I would do would make any difference.

"I Am Not Lovable"

❏ I often worry that the person I'm in a love relationship with will stop loving me or find someone they love more.

❏ I don't deeply believe that I am capable of having a truly fulfilling, satisfying love relationship.

❏ I have a pattern of getting into relationships with people who reject me or leave me.

❏ I sometimes push away the people I love most, and I can't figure out why.

❏ I sometimes smother the people I love most, and I can't figure out why.

❏ Even though I know my spouse is faithful to me, I can't help having strong feelings of jealousy.

❏ I am afraid to commit to a relationship, even with someone I know I love, because I can't shake the fear that they will eventually betray me or leave me.

❏ I feel like I have been too damaged by my past for anyone to truly love me.

"I Cannot Trust Anyone."

- ❏ I am afraid or unwilling to trust men/women/anyone in authority/my colleagues or partners/and so forth.
- ❏ I am afraid or unwilling to trust people in general.
- ❏ People I am close with tell me I am overly controlling, that I have to do everything myself to feel like it's done correctly.
- ❏ My kids/spouse are starting to resent me because they say I always tell them what to do/don't trust them.
- ❏ I tend to have a hard time having fun, letting down, or relaxing among friends.
- ❏ My wife/husband says I am not spontaneous.
- ❏ I feel like I have an "opposite Midas touch"—everything I touch turns to muck.
- ❏ I am afraid to get close to anyone or really show them my feelings.
- ❏ I have a hard time trusting my own judgment.

"I Am Bad."

- ❏ I feel like a terrible person.
- ❏ I am always expecting the worst.
- ❏ Whenever something good happens, I can't enjoy it because I'm waiting for the other shoe to drop.
- ❏ I feel guilty about things I've done in the past.
- ❏ I feel guilty, even though I don't know exactly what I have to feel guilty about.
- ❏ I feel like the people around me would be better off without me here.
- ❏ I have a hard time expecting anything to turn out well.
- ❏ I have a long pattern of self-sabotage in my work/my relationships/my health/my life.
- ❏ I feel like other people are better than I am.

❏ I can't shake the feeling that there's something
fundamentally wrong with me, that I'm a bad person.

"I Am Alone."

❏ Even when I'm surrounded by others, I feel alone.
❏ I have the sense that nobody could possibly understand me
or how I feel.
❏ I have a hard time believing there is such a thing as a soul, or
that if there is, that I have one.
❏ I have this feeling that I don't belong here.
❏ Sometimes it just doesn't feel like life is worth living.
❏ Life feels to me sometimes like one big joke, or one big
tragedy.
❏ Life feels meaningless to me.
❏ I am angry at God/angry at myself.

"What if I'm not sure which belief most fits me?" people sometimes
ask.

There is no wrong answer here. Again, the Four-Step Process is a
very forgiving system. Even if you select a belief that doesn't coincide
perfectly with what you actually believe, you're going to get improvement anyway. It isn't like taking the wrong medicine: it's *all* the right
medicine. One or two beliefs will more accurately describe your own
situation than others and will give you a more direct line to the core
issues you're dealing with.

But *any* of them will get you there.

No matter which belief you select to start the process with, you are
going to activate the same parts of the brain and move in a general way
from "There's something wrong with me" to "There's something right
with me." Irrespective of the details and particular slant of your own
version of self-limiting belief, it's going to create results.

So . . . that should be that, right? Once you have identified the false, self-limiting belief structures that have been affecting your perceptions, now that you know where they may have come from and that they are not the way reality truly is, now that you know what's going on in there, you can just say to yourself, "Okay, that was then—and this is now. I'm over it!"

Right?

Not quite.

Of course, it's not so simple. If that were all there was to it, then Stefanie would never have come to see us. If that were all there was to it, then you would not be reading this book, and we would have had no reason for writing it.

Just because you identify a false, self-limiting belief doesn't mean you don't still feel it. As we said before, simply knowing it isn't enough: that fog of distress resists logic. Talking it through is no more effective than trying to change the channel of a television set by shouting at it.

Exactly why is that true? Why do these beliefs persist and hold such a powerful sway over our lives?

That's what the next chapter is all about.

3

The Flea and the Elephant

I do not understand what I do. For what I want
to do, I do not do—but what I hate, I do.
—The Apostle Paul, in *Epistle to the Romans* 7:15 (NIV)

ONCE UPON A TIME there was a flea who believed that he was king of the world.

One day he decided that he wanted to go to the beach for a swim. But the western shore was many miles away, and on his own, the flea could travel only inches at a time. If he was going to reach the shore during his lifetime, he would need transportation.

So he called out to his elephant. "Ho there, Elephant, let's go out!"

The flea's elephant came to his side and kneeled down. The flea hopped up and, pointing to the west, said, "That way—to the beach!"

But the elephant did not go west. He rather felt like taking a stroll in the forest to the east, and that is what he did. The flea, much to his dismay, could do nothing but go along for the ride, and spent the day being smacked in the face by leaves and branches.

The next day, the flea tried to get the elephant to take him to the store to buy salve for his face. Instead, the elephant took a long romp in the northern mountains, terrifying the poor flea so badly that he could not sleep that night. The flea stayed in his bed for days, beset by nightmares of thundering along mountain roads, certain he would fall to his death, and awoke each morning in a cold sweat.

After a week, finally feeling well enough to rise from his bed, the flea beckoned the elephant to his side, clambered up, and said, "I'm not well. Please, take me to the doctor."

But the elephant merrily trundled off to the western seashore, where he spent the day swimming. The flea nearly drowned.

That night, sitting by the fireplace and trying to warm himself, the flea had a thought. He turned to the elephant and said, "About tomorrow . . . um, what are *your* plans?"

You're probably wondering what the moral of this story is. It is simply this: if you are a flea riding an elephant, before you make any plans, you might want to check out what your elephant has in mind.

This point is more important to your life than it might seem—because in fact, you *are* a flea riding an elephant. The flea of the story represents your *conscious mind*, which includes your intellect and power of reason, your ambitions and aspirations, your ideas, thoughts, hopes, and plans. In short, everything you think of as *you*. And the elephant? That's your *subconscious mind*.

To understand how these two work together—or don't, as is often the case—let's start with the flea.

Your Brilliant, Amazing Conscious Mind

The human brain is the most remarkable, versatile, powerful creation we know of. Its roughly 100 billion neuron cells pass messages to one another through as many as one quadrillion connections—several thousand times the number of all the known celestial bodies in the Milky Way galaxy. The human brain's capacity, to put it mildly, is enormous.

Carefully couched within its bony shell, floating in an amniotic-like bath of cerebrospinal fluid atop the impact-cushioning spinal structure, everything about the brain is designed to give it maximum nourishment, care, and protection. Weighing two to three pounds, your brain comprises a mere 1 to 2 percent of your total body weight, yet it consumes 15 percent of your total blood flow, 20 percent of the air you breathe, and some 20 to 30 percent of your body's total energy intake.

In an average adult brain, approximately 100,000 miles of myelinated axons (functional nerve fibers) are wound like an incredibly complex ball of yarn into a structure resembling a pair of clenched fists. In fact, if you want to get a fair sense of the size and shape of your brain, make two fists right now and hold them up together, knuckles to knuckles.

At its core and base (thumbs, palms, and fingertips) lie the cerebellum, amygdalae, hippocampus, brain stem, and other structures that are in charge of hundreds of thousands of automatic functions, such as balance and motor skills, managing sensory input, and the stress response actions we mentioned in chapter 1. The layers of tissue wrapped around the front and top of the brain (fingers and knuckles), the part involved in conscious thought, is called the *prefrontal cortex* or *frontal lobe*.

The frontal lobe is the CEO of the brain, responsible for focus and concentration, for learning and the power of conscious observation. This is the part of the brain that thinks and reasons, the part through which you evaluate options, make new decisions, and exercise your free will. It is the part of you that is reading these words right now, while your brain stem and other more primal centers maintain your breathing, heartbeat, and a myriad of other functions well below the radar of your conscious awareness. If you imagine your body as a gigantic ocean vessel, your frontal lobe is the captain. It decides where you want to go, charts the course, and gives the orders that the thousands of crew members then carry out. This is the conscious brain, the part we think of as "me."

The frontal lobe is the crown jewel of the human brain. More than our opposable thumbs, bifocal vision, or any other trait, it is the size of our frontal lobe in relation to the rest of our brain that distinguishes us from other animal species. Frontal lobes in history have penned the words of Shakespeare, the music of Bach, the inventions of Leonardo.

However, for all its brilliance, the conscious brain has its limits—and those limits turn out to be pretty severe.

George Miller, Ph.D., one of the founding fathers of modern cognitive psychology and an authority on human perception, was the first to describe the workings of the brain as an information processor—essentially, a living computer. Dr. Miller's most famous contribution to cognitive science was the concept of *chunking,* an aspect of short-term memory. According to Miller, our short-term (that is, conscious) memory is capable of holding about seven "chunks" of information at any one time: for example, seven words, chess positions, faces, or digits. (Dr. Miller's discovery is sometimes cited as the rationale behind Bell Telephone's decision to standardize phone numbers as seven digits in length.) It's something like the juggler spinning plates atop those slender sticks: if the conscious brain tries to hold on to many more than seven details at one time, you will soon see some broken plates on the floor.

But look at what else is going on that the brain has to keep track of! There are millions of physiological processes happening in the body, processes that, if they were to falter or stop altogether, would leave us impaired or dead. Cell metabolism, heart and circulatory function, endocrine adjustments, sensory input (and its simultaneous evaluation for signs of danger), smooth muscle operation at hundreds of thousands of different sites around the body . . . the scope of the task is staggering. Imagine having to give conscious attention to every single metabolic reaction happening within our digestion and endocrine glands. If the conscious mind were in charge of all these processes, we wouldn't last ten minutes.

Fortunately, the conscious mind is *not* the one in charge of it all.

An Undiscovered Continent

The concept of a *subconscious* mind is a fairly recent thing, although humans have always sensed there was some deeper, unseen force there, lying underneath, behind, or beyond the conscious mind. Since the ancient Greeks, scientists have struggled to figure out exactly how to view the human *psyche*, a Greek word meaning "mind" or "soul." Aristotle talked about the imagination (*phantasia*), as distinct from perception and mind, implying that it was a space within the mind that worked with specific images (*phantasma*) and combined them to arrive at abstract ideas. Mythologies of all cultures are rich with stories of people tapping a greater wisdom through the imagery arising in their dreams.

During the European Renaissance and "Age of Reason," the conscious mind was especially exalted. René Descartes's famous philosophical statement, "I think, therefore I am," was in part a declaration of the clarity and pure self-awareness of human thought. Several generations later, John Locke's *Essay Concerning Human Understanding* further championed the idea of man's complete and transparent self-awareness. But this neat, orderly view did not hold water for long. "At the end of the [nineteenth] century," as Tor Norretrander writes in *The User Illusion*, "the notion of the transparent man was severely challenged," as scientists continued to push the envelope of their observations of the human animal. "Hermann Helmholtz, the German physicist and physiologist, began studying human reactions around 1850 . . . [and] concluded that most of what took place in our heads was unconscious."

By the end of the nineteenth century, scientists including William James, Arthur Schopenhauer, and Pierre Janet were using the terms *unconscious* and *subconscious* in their efforts to explore this territory. It was Sigmund Freud, in his 1899 *The Interpretation of Dreams*, who most famously recognized that there was a vast and uncharted continent within the human mind that had a huge impact on our lives. Calling it the *unconscious mind*, Freud began the task of charting this unknown landscape, using what tools he had at his disposal, largely consisting of verbal dialogue and the analysis of dreams, which he termed the "royal road to the unconscious." (While the term *unconscious* is still generally preferred in scientific circles and Freud himself publically condemned the term *subconscious,* the latter term has come to be more widely used in everyday language, so we have opted to use it in this book.)

Freud's conception of the unconscious mind was generally negative, in the sense that he viewed it as the repository for socially unacceptable wishes and desires, painful and repressed memories, and the like. His contemporaries, notably Pierre Janet and Carl Jung, developed this idea in further directions, as have many different schools of psychology since that time. However, the basic tools of investigation available to these generations of researchers and clinicians did not change or improve significantly—until the 1990s, with the advent of high-tech methods of brain imaging and especially functional magnetic resonance imaging (fMRI).

One of the many advantages gained from the new imaging technology was that, unlike the tools of electroencephalography (EEG) and magnetoencephalography (MEG), which were significantly limited to measuring activity near the surface of the brain, the fMRI allowed researchers to look deep within the interior of the brain, paving the way for a new understanding of the sheer scope and complexity of what goes on deep inside our heads. It was as if we had spent a century attempting to explore an entire continent on foot and had suddenly gained access to helicopters, airplanes, and satellite photography.

And what an extraordinary picture it was that began to emerge! The subconscious mind:

- Is responsible for all the thousands of processes and subprocesses of physiological metabolism, functions of which the conscious brain is almost completely oblivious
- Manages and sorts through millions of bits per second of sensory input, of which our conscious brain is aware of only the tiniest slice
- Files, sorts, and maintains a storehouse of memories that, while scientists have still not fully been able to quantify it, probably numbers in the trillions

• Manages bodily functions our conscious brain typically ignores, including the minute and complex details of movement and balance, breathing, blinking, use of hands and fingers, the coordinated complexes of motion involved in walking, talking, driving a car, and so forth

George Miller, who gave us the concept of chunking, also quantified the difference between the operational capacity of the conscious mind and the subconscious mind. According to Dr. Miller, the conscious mind puts out on average between 20 and 40 neuron firings per second, while the subconscious puts out between 20 and 40 *million* firings per second. In other words, in measuring the activity of the subconscious mind as compared to the conscious mind, we're looking at a factor of about a million to one.

Which turns out to be roughly the ratio of an elephant's weight to that of, you guessed it, a flea.

An Iceberg Beneath the Surface

On one wall of our office there hangs a large photo of an iceberg to remind us of this reality of human nature.

On average, roughly one-tenth of an iceberg's mass appears above water level, which means that about 90 percent of it is below the water's surface. This is something like how the human mind is arranged, only here the numbers are quite different. In terms of physical tissue, about 15 percent of the brain's mass is dedicated to conscious processes: close to tip-of-the-iceberg proportions. But in terms of bits of information processing, the conscious mind's function represents one *ten-thousandth of one percent* of the brain's total function.

The brain, in other words, is an iceberg that is 99.9999 percent submerged below our level of conscious awareness.

We can access tiny bits of that submerged portion when we want—for example, when we want to remember what it was we meant to get at the store as we walk its aisles. (Because of chunking, though, if it's more than about seven items, it might be best to make a list before you go!) Pulling up a picture in your mind's eye of someone you knew in school, or the house where you grew up. Remembering a phone number.

But you cannot pull up *all* the phone numbers you know, or the faces of *everyone* you have ever met, even though they are all in there in the mostly submerged iceberg of your mind. If you could pull all that up at once, your conscious brain would be so flooded with information it would be overwhelmed and useless. It *has* to focus in order to function.

The conscious mind concentrates on a very narrow spectrum of what is going on in our lives at any given moment. It has the capacity to shift that focus and to initiate a new action—but it typically does not stay involved in the majority of the steps that are involved in *taking* that action. When you decide to recall something—that phone number, that face from the past—your conscious mind initiates the search. Like the captain on the bridge of an aircraft carrier, it gives the command, but then the command itself is carried out by the crew, that is, your subconscious.

Using your conscious mind is something like standing in the middle of a vast museum at night with all the lights off. There you stand, in pitch blackness, and your conscious mind is the pencil-thin beam of a penlight: you can shine it on any one shelf, any one exhibit, but not on all of them at once.

Which means it can be difficult to know what we really believe.

Beliefs are large patterns of thought. If thoughts themselves are the rush of rainfall down a mountainside, beliefs are the channels in the ground through which the water runs. As we saw in chapter 2, we form our beliefs by building new neural tissue and synaptic connections. To a great extent, they live in the subconscious brain. They are thought subroutines. Like breathing, we can put the focus of our attention on a belief if we try, but 99.9999 percent of the time, like our breathing, we don't think about our beliefs; we just let them *run*.

Normally, this works out just fine. But when we have formed beliefs that are in direct conflict with our conscious desires, intentions, values, and goals in life, then, Houston, we have a problem. Because, while the flea may want to go west, if the elephant decides to go east or north, there isn't much we can do but go along for the ride—and as the flea discovered, the ride can be brutal.

Of Two Minds

The subconscious mind works largely by association. It connects things to other things. In other words, it pays attention to resonance—and it is always working in the background. This means that when we have an experience in our conscious awareness, our subconscious is busy in the background looking for past experiences that resonate with it or that are in some way similar. It's saying, "What can we draw on to help us deal with this situation?"

Some of this comparative thinking may surface to the level of conscious awareness. Most of it, though, occurs so deep in the subconscious that we aren't aware of it, and thus we may find ourselves reacting to situations in ways that don't seem to make any logical sense to us. (Like Clay, the airline pilot hugging the carpet.)

This is the reason the powerful experiences of our early lives can hold such a powerful sway over our present lives: while the flea of our conscious mind pays attention to what is happening right now, the elephant of our subconscious mind is continuously referring back to whatever is familiar in the vast files of our past. Even if the associations or connections are not that easy to see, the subconscious mind is programmed to find those similarities, and it's extremely clever at doing so.

From a survival standpoint, this strategy makes perfect sense: the best predictor of the future is past experience. If we catch whiff of a scent, sound, or sight that is reminiscent of that hungry tiger we encountered years ago, it's very useful to pull that memory back out of storage instantly and get those alert messages shooting into the amygdalae and adrenals as quickly as possible. The subconscious can act about a million times faster than the conscious mind—and *it does.*

But this refer-and-alert strategy is not so helpful if the original information was distorted. Garbage in, garbage out, as computer programmers used to say. If you have a flaw in the original assumption, then anything you base on that assumption will be flawed as well. Thus, if we built a belief based on traumatic or microtraumatic childhood experiences that said, *Everyone I get close to will abandon me,* or, *I am a fraud and a failure,* then those are the files our elephant refers to in deciding which way he goes.

Again, the subconscious is extremely adept at finding these clues. The ratio of what we *sense*—that is, what our subconscious mind takes in—to what we consciously *perceive* is about one million to one. That's a lot of information. And if your conscious perceptions and your subconscious conclusions are not in alignment, guess which one overrules the other?

For example, let's talk about relationships.

You meet someone new. First thing that happens, even before you smile and say, "Can I get that door for you?" is that your subconscious mind is processing millions of bits of information at lightning speed, hunting for all possible similarities between this person and this encounter with everyone and every other encounter in your entire past experience—physical traits, facial expressions, mannerisms, clothing, vocabulary, scents, sounds, anything—and then shooting mini-conclusions to the inner portions of your brain: *he's not safe, you can't trust him, he might betray you, he slurs his T's just like that kid who made fun of you in third grade, his eyebrows are just like your dad's—and remember how your dad always criticized you . . .*

You are most likely not conscious of any of this, but it shades your perceptions in subtle ways—often *very* subtle. Consciously, you're thinking, "Hey, he seems like a nice guy." Subconsciously, millions of synapses are screaming, *Don't get close to this guy, you can't trust him, he'll hurt you!*

Suddenly you are the flea, thinking you are going to the beach with a new friend—and the elephant is galloping off toward the forest in the opposite direction. And the same thing happens not only in romantic relationships but also in business dealings, in classrooms, in friendships, in human interactions of every type and in every context.

This sheds new light on what happened with Stefanie. The greatest source of difficulty for Stefanie was that she consciously intended to move in one direction, but her subconscious beliefs were taking her in the opposite direction.

You can see the conflict back in her original childhood experience. Trotting home with her quarter in hand, she felt pleased and proud—until her parents' reaction gave her the message that she should have felt ashamed of what she did, not proud. A similar conflict was alive and well in her as an adult. On the one hand, she worked hard to succeed in her business, her community, and her family life, achieving what she regarded as noble aims—but on the other hand, there was a message still hovering there that said something like, "Whatever it is you *think* you should be proud of, you should *really* be ashamed of it."

The flea of Stefanie's educated, skilled, very intelligent consciousness was all about creating a successful business that would benefit not only her family but thousands of others as well, making a wonderful contribution to society in the process.

But that's not the direction her elephant wanted to walk.

Remember Clay, the fighter pilot who was terrified of heights? Clay's flea was perfectly happy to dine out at the rotating restaurant on the top floor of a tall hotel in his neighborhood. His elephant refused to go near the place.

Using a common expression, we might say of Stefanie that she was "of two minds" concerning success, and that Clay was "of two minds" concerning whether it was safe to be suspended up in the air. And in both cases, this would be the literal truth—two minds: one conscious, one subconscious. The flea and the elephant.

This is why the Four-Step Process starts by asking the exact same question that the flea of our story finally hit on: Which way is that elephant headed? What do we truly, deeply *believe*?

How Do We Know Where the Elephant Is Headed?

Steve Hopkins has always been such a naturally friendly and sociable guy, you'd never have known he had a problem, but he certainly did.

"When we go out to dinner," his wife explained as they sat together in our office, "Steve calls ahead to the restaurant to make sure they have our meals ready when we get there. He wants to go in, eat, and get out again as quickly as possible."

"It's not that I *want* to," added Steve. "I *have* to."

A high-ranking sales director with a large, successful company and on his way up in the world, Steve was in a position that required him to interact with people continually. His clients never suspected anything out of the ordinary was going on, but on the inside, Steve suffered through every social event he attended. Whether it was with colleagues, potential clients, or family and friends, Steve desperately wanted to get into the restaurant and out again without spending any more time there than was absolutely necessary. Ideally, he'd be out in minutes and in bed by 8:30.

"I know it drives my wife and my kids crazy," he said. "Almost as soon as we get somewhere, I'm calling it quits and have to leave. I know it's strange, and I have no idea where it comes from. It's just how I am."

Steve's elephant was calling the shots, and it was making him miserable. So just where was that elephant headed, and why?

Using a technique we will explore in just a moment, we identified that something significant may have happened to Steve some time between sixth and seventh grade.

"Oh, I know exactly what this was," he said. "We moved."

When Steve was eleven his family moved to a new house in a different neighborhood and he began attending a different school. Suddenly he went from being popular to being unknown and alone. Fairly short for his age, he was immediately picked on, and because none of the other kids knew him yet, nobody stuck up for him.

This chapter in Steve's life did not last forever. Naturally sociable even at that age, Steve was able to adapt and before long had made new friends. But the experience was an asteroid strike that left its mark, and now, as an adult, he was completely panicked about going out into social situations. That eleven-year-old experience was still telling him that he might be picked on and ridiculed.

A classic case of *I'm not safe.*

We took him through the Four-Step Process. His wife called the next day. "We went to a restaurant last night," she said excitedly, "and we sat down, ate, and talked—for over an *hour.*" We continued working with Steve, going back and sorting out a number of distinct early events and dissipating their impact, one by one. A few weeks later his daughter reported, "It's amazing to see my dad go out socially. We just went out with a group of thirty people the other night—and he lasted all evening!"

Steve soon reported an economic fringe benefit to his new sense of well-being. Because flying commercial airlines had always caused him so much anxiety, he had been spending a small fortune on chartered jets whenever he and his wife had to travel—money he now no longer needed to spend.

Case closed . . . except that here is where it gets really curious. One day Steve called us to report another change, one he had not anticipated.

Some thirty years earlier, Steve had fallen off a roof during a thunderstorm and broken his neck. Miraculously, he was not paralyzed, and he soon regained full use of his limbs, but he had continued to have problems with his back and neck ever since. Despite working with chiropractors, orthopedic doctors, everyone he could think of, he had been unable to get full relief, and the pain had continued to plague him.

Until now.

"I don't know what you did," he told us, "but that chronic pain in my neck and back? It's *gone*."

Of course, it wasn't what *we* did, it was what *he* did: he identified and cleared the trauma, which allowed his fog of distress to finally dissipate.

The problem had been that, while the injury from his fall had healed, the echo of the trauma had not. In the few seconds it took for that terrible accident to occur, an asteroid of fear had ripped through Steve's being: fear of the fall, fear of dying, fear for his family. His muscles had stored the emotional trauma associated with the injury to that area, and while the event itself was over in moments and the obvious effects of the injury had healed in months, the echo of all of that emotional impact was still encoded in the fabric of Steve's neuromusculature all these decades later. And, as with David the journalist, working on one issue had also relieved an entirely different issue—because to the subconscious, it was *not* entirely different, but just another resonant facet of the same issue: *I'm not safe.*

There was nothing wrong with Steve's neck muscles, physiologically. But they knew something Steve's conscious mind did not: they knew what was on the elephant's mind.

They were *part* of the elephant's mind.

Candace Pert, Ph.D., who served for twenty years as section chief on brain chemistry of the clinical neuroscience branch at the National Institutes of Health, is a leading researcher on the relationship of physical and emotional health and trauma.

"People have a hard time discriminating between physical and mental pain," says Dr. Pert. "Often we are stuck in an unpleasant emotional event from the past that is stored at every level of our nervous system and even on the cellular level. My laboratory research has suggested that all the senses—sight, sound, smell, taste, and touch—are filtered, and memories stored, through the *molecules of emotions,* mostly the neuropeptides and their receptors, at every level of the bodymind."

Scientists generally believed that neuropeptides predominately populated the brain, until Dr. Pert and other researchers demonstrated that we have similar neural receptor cells running throughout our bodies, or to put it another way, that intelligence resides throughout our bodies, and not exclusively within the cranium. And that intelligence knows a great deal more than our conscious minds *know* it knows.

In a sense, muscle memory is really an aspect of our subconscious intelligence. The working of the subconscious, in other words, is not limited exclusively to certain parts of the brain alone but is distributed throughout the body. The muscles and other tissues of the body are, functionally speaking, part of the subconscious mind.

And we can use that body intelligence to learn what our subconscious is really thinking.

Your Body Knows

You're probably wondering, just how did we suspect that something had happened to Steve when he was in sixth or seventh grade? We used a technique we call *neuromuscular feedback.*

Often referred to as *muscle testing* or *applied kinesiology,* this simple process can tap into a tremendous amount of information that the person being tested may not be consciously aware of, from details on the subject's health and current state of mind to particulars about his or her own history and family dynamics.

One thing we love about this technique is the utter simplicity of the premise. The basic idea is that the body has an unerringly accurate and complete self-knowledge. On a very primal level, we know a good deal more about ourselves than we think we know. Our sophisticated conscious mind may not have access to that enormous body of knowledge, but our muscles and peripheral nerves do.

In a way, this is common sense. We reveal it in our language. For example, when we are about to give someone some emotionally charged news, whether very good or very bad, we say, "Are you sitting down?" Why? Because we know instinctively that a strong surge of emotion can make our muscles suddenly go slack. You're probably familiar with the texting shorthand LOL ROTF—*laughing out loud, rolling on the floor.* In the days before text messaging was popular, we used to say, "I fell out of my chair laughing."

These are more than mere figures of speech. Strong emotional responses do have instant echoes in our neuromusculature. In fact, scientific studies have shown that the stress evoked by making an untrue statement consistently causes a weakening of the muscles of anywhere from 5 to 15 percent. This is not a huge difference, but it's distinct enough to be clearly discernable. What's more, this happens whether or not the person being tested knows *consciously* that the statement is false.

The conscious mind can play tricks on us—but the body always tells the truth.

As a simple overview, here is how neuromuscular feedback works: you make a declarative statement while holding out your arm, and the person testing you presses down with mild but firm pressure. If your statement is true, your arm will resist the tester's push and remain in place. But if your statement is false—*whether or not you are consciously aware of it*—your arm will weaken slightly and give in to the tester's downward push.

Neuromuscular feedback opens a window to a whole new world of information. Bypassing years of conscious thoughts, concepts, and opinions, it directly reveals our mostly deeply held subconscious beliefs as conveyed through our peripheral nerves and muscles.

Window to the Truth

In our earlier description of that first office visit with Stefanie, we left out one key detail: before going through all her history, we took a few minutes to do some neuromuscular feedback.

When Stefanie's arm was outstretched, we said, "Something upsetting happened to you when you were five or younger." Her arm weakened and lowered, giving in to our mild downward pressure, meaning *Not true—nothing profoundly upsetting happened when I was five or younger.*

"When you were six," we continued. Another weakening of the arm: no, not at that age either. "When you were seven." *Bingo*. Stefanie's arm now held solid, indicating a resounding *yes*. Whatever upsetting event it was we were looking for had happened at the age of seven, and her neuromusculature knew it.

Once we had pinpointed the exact age when that asteroid hit Stefanie's world, she immediately knew what event we were talking about.

As far as Stefanie was concerned, that event surrounding the quarter her aunt had given her was something from her childhood, something long behind her. No big deal, yesterday's news. But it was *not* yesterday's news: her nerve and muscle fibers were still shaking with the emotional impact of the experience. Her conscious mind said, "Hey, no big deal," but her body was screaming out, "It's a *huge* big deal—I'm still upset about it!"

We are all well defended; that's how we get by. Our remarkable capacity for self-deception allows us to deny reality in order to feel more comfortable in the moment. Neuromuscular feedback slips behind the curtain of denial, behind the façade that says, "Oh, I got over that a long time ago," and sees clearly what is truly going on deep inside ourselves.

A little later in that same visit, we did some additional neuromuscular feedback to help Stefanie more vividly see what we were seeing. We had her make the statement, "I am CEO of [her company's name]," and she tested strong. No surprise there. Then we had her make this statement: "I want to be financially successful"—and much to her astonishment, *her arm went weak*.

We tested her on this: "I want my family to be happy." She tested strong. It was true. Her flea and her elephant were in agreement: they both wanted *that*. But when we had her then say, "*I* want to be happy," her arm went weak. Her flea wanted her to be happy. Her elephant had other ideas.

How to Do Basic Neuromuscular Feedback

To give yourself a simple demonstration of neuromuscular feedback, all you need is a few minutes together with a willing partner to serve as tester. Your partner does not need to know any background or detail; all they have to do is follow these simple instructions. (We have also provided a brief instructional video on this book's website: www.codetojoy .com.)

1. First neutralize the system. ⚡

In order to ensure that you get accurate results, it is helpful for both the *subject* (you) and the *tester* (your friend) to first take a minute to balance your neuromuscular system with a simple breathing exercise. We call this *crosshand breathing,* and here is how you do it:

- In a seated position, cross your left ankle over your right.
- Place your left hand across your chest, so that the fingers rest over the right side of your collarbone. Then cross your right hand over your left, so that the fingers of your right hand rest over the left side of your collarbone.
- Breathe in through your nose and out through your mouth. As you breathe in, let your tongue touch the roof of your mouth, just behind your front teeth. As you breathe out again, let your tongue rest behind your lower front teeth.

Continue breathing this way, slow, even, and relaxed, for about two minutes.

Crosshand Breathing

You'll find this not only helps to ensure accurate results in what follows, it also is likely to make you feel significantly clearer and more relaxed. We'll return to this exercise in the next chapter and learn more about exactly what it and other similar exercises do in the body, and why.

For now, though, let's go on to master the basics of neuromuscular feedback.

2. Get the feel of it.

To begin, the two of you stand facing each other. You (the subject) hold one arm straight out to your side, palm down. While you continue holding your arm out straight, your partner (the tester) places the fingers of one hand on top of your wrist and pushes down, gently but firmly, while you resist the downward pressure and try to keep your arm straight.

At first, the tester presses down just firmly enough to feel the extent of your resistance. Neither of you should lock your arm or make an effort to be forceful. Think of this as *calibrating the instrument:* you're

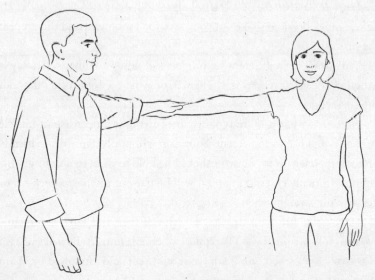

Neuromuscular Feedback

finding out just how much force it takes to match the tester's downward push with the subject's resistance.

It does not matter whether you use your right or left arm. If either arm has any sort of soreness or physical problem, simply use the other arm.

3. Test a true statement.

Have your partner test you while you say, "My name is . . . ," and state your true name. You should be able easily to maintain your arm straight out as before.

4. Test a false statement.

Now have your partner test you again while you say, "My name is . . . ," and this time substitute some other name, not your own. In other words, lie. Typically your muscle will be sufficiently weakened that it will not be able to resist the tester's downward push, and your arm will give way.

5. Test another set of true/false statements.

Take a quick break to shake out your arm for a moment, and then repeat the process.

This time, try a different set of true and false statements: "Today is Monday," or whatever day it is. Then, "Today is . . ." some other day, not the correct day.

Note that what you are typically measuring is a decrease in muscle strength of only 5 to 15 percent. Your arm will not collapse dramatically or go completely limp. But you should be able to discern a definite difference. In many cases, the subject will be flat-out unable to keep his or her arm out straight when "testing weak."

Have some fun with this; try a series of true and false statements. For example, we often use "Two plus two equals four," followed by "Two plus two equals seven," or "I am [your age] years old" followed by "I am [some other age] years old."

You don't want to overdo it to the point where you tire or strain your arm. But play with it enough to get the feel of the difference between testing strong and testing weak. Again, this is not a test of wills; neither tester nor subject should exert a major effort. The point is not for the tester to force your arm down, but for you both to work together to gauge your arm's ability to resist.

Now, let's use this tool to investigate what's going on for you at a subconscious level. You'll notice that in our meeting with Stefanie, we used neuromuscular feedback twice: once to pinpoint her negative past experience, and once to pinpoint her self-limiting belief. Let's now do the same with you, starting with pinpointing that past event.

Using Neuromuscular Feedback to Identify Significant Past Experiences

As you went through chapter 1, you identified a number of events and experiences in your past that may be having a long-term negative impact on your life. You can use neuromuscular feedback to determine which events are most relevant to your current issue or problem.

There may be a number of significant events, but let's seek to identify the *single most significant* one, that is, the one experience that has had the strongest negative impact on you.

Starting with your list of significant past events, which you wrote out in chapter 1, now test each event, just as you tested simple statements about your name or the date.

> "*Grandma died* has a significant impact on my present problem."
>
> "*Grandma died* does *not* have a significant impact on my present problem."

Make sure these are statements, and not questions. Each statement you test should be in the form of a present tense, declarative statement: "This is so," or "This is not so."

Once you have identified which events are significant, you can refine your search further:

> *"Grandma died* is having the strongest negative influence in my life right now."

> *"Grandma died* is *not* having the strongest negative influence in my life right now."

In chapter 1, we suggested that you identify each significant negative past event with just a few words. Now you can see how useful this is. It's far easier to test statements that are short and simple rather than lengthy and involved.

For simplicity's sake, it is helpful to narrow your search here down to a single past event. Of course, there may well be more than one such event that has had an impact on you, and in time, you can certainly work through all of them. But as you go through the Four-Step Process for your first time, it is helpful to focus on just one past event.

Later, you can come back and go through the process a second time, focusing on a second past event, and a third, and as many times as you want. In Stefanie's case, we helped her go through and clear three distinct past events, one at a time. In Steve Hopkins's case, it was six.

But for now, find one to focus on.

Using Neuromuscular Feedback to Identify Your Self-Limiting Beliefs

Once you have gone through the events of your past, you can use the same process to assess the self-limiting beliefs you worked with in chapter 2.

> *"I am not safe* is my strongest self-limiting belief."

> *"I am not safe* is *not* my strongest self-limiting belief."

And so on.

As with the testing of significant past events, you may find more than one self-limiting belief. In fact, chances are good that you will. Most people are dealing with not one but at least two or three of these beliefs. But again, it is most helpful to single out the *one most significant* belief and work on just that one for now.

Again, as we said in chapter 2, there are no wrong answers here: the Four-Step Process is a very forgiving system. Even if you select a belief that doesn't perfectly match what is truly going on for you, you're going to get improvement anyway. It's just that the more accurately you pinpoint the events that have affected you and the beliefs that are affecting you now, the more rapid and dramatic that improvement will tend to be.

Does This Really Work?

"How do I know this is really working, and the other person isn't just pushing harder on my arm?" People often ask us this. After all, couldn't this just be an example of the placebo effect—all in our minds?

It's a reasonable question. We wondered the same thing ourselves when we first began exploring the process many years ago. But the results of neuromuscular feedback are objectively measurable by the tools and instruments of hard science.

One of the most striking confirmations of neuromuscular feedback appeared more than a decade ago, in a 1999 study conducted by Daniel Monti, M.D., a professor at Philadelphia's Jefferson Medical College. Monti and his colleagues took a group of eighty-nine medical students and systematically had them say true and false statements. (In the language of the study, they were "exposed to congruous and incongruous semantic stimuli.")

There was no human factor involved in making the measurements. Instead, they used computerized dynamometers (an instrument that measures power output) to measure the force exerted on the subjects' deltoid (shoulder) muscles. Muscle response, as measured by these purely objective physical instruments, was consistently some *17 percent weaker* when the subjects made incongruous (that is, false) statements.

As we mentioned, this process is not meant to be a test of brute strength. Still, we once had an interesting opportunity to test the sheer physical limits of the procedure when we had a visit from one of the world's strongest athletes, whom we will call Dan.

A former NFL lineman, Dan ranked at the time as the number two power lifter in the world. He had flown in from the East Coast to participate in an international competition in California. During his visit, we asked if we might do some simple neuromuscular feedback, and he readily agreed.

Dan was the biggest man either of us had ever seen up close. When he held out his arm for us to test, it felt like we were putting our hand on a tree trunk. At our direction, he stated his name. Not surprisingly, we could not budge his arm. (The man has the power of a horse.) Then, again at our direction, he again stated what his name was, but this time he gave a fictitious identity. We easily pushed his arm down.

He couldn't believe it. He was convinced it was a trick. "Let me try that again," he said. We did. This time, he tried with all his might to keep his arm outstretched. He simply could not do it.

That is the beauty of muscle testing: it's simple, and it *works*.

Trouble-Shooting

"What if my tester can't feel any difference?"

Make sure your tester waits just a moment after you make the statement, before gently applying pressure. Also make sure this is gentle, gradual downward pressure, and not an immediate or abrupt pushing.

"What if our results seem unclear or inconsistent?"

Make sure you are focusing on the statement you are testing, and not simply saying it out loud while thinking about something or someone else. Neuromuscular feedback will work just as well whether you speak your statement out loud or simply think it silently—so if you are thinking strongly about something else while you make a verbal statement, it could confuse the results.

It's best for subject and tester not to look each other in the eye while testing, as it's too easy for the tester to look for subtle cues in the subject's face. The tester should strive to be a neutral agent here, acting purely as an objective, mechanical arm.

If you have concerns about the tester's objectivity concerning your past events and limiting beliefs, or if you feel uncomfortable speaking these various beliefs out loud in front of your tester, you can always test these statements by making them silently. In that case, you can tell the tester you will make a silent statement in your mind, and that you will nod to them when it's time for them to test. This way, they will not even know what statement they are testing.

"What if our answers come out backward—for example, if 'Two plus two equals seven' tests strong instead of weak?"

If you're getting a clear distinction, but it's opposite from what it should be, then have both of you sit and do another two minutes of crosshand breathing to ensure that your systems are balanced and neutral.

If you are still not getting clear results after doing this, then leave it for now and go on to the next chapter. We will look at more techniques for clearing and balancing your system in chapter 4, and you may want to wait until you go through those and then come back to explore neuromuscular feedback at that point.

"What if I don't have anyone I can get to be my testing partner?"

Although it takes time and practice, it is possible to act as your own tester. We have provided an overview of how to do this on our website, www.codetojoy.com.

However, it's also important to understand that, while neuromuscular feedback is a powerful and valuable tool, it isn't absolutely essential here. If you don't have anyone to partner with at the moment, you can still effectively practice every step of the Four-Step Process.

In fact, there are three basic tools you have that will help you gauge which are the specific past negative events and present self-limiting beliefs you want to deal with:

1. The evidence of your life

To an extent, we can see what our deeply held beliefs are simply by looking at the results in our lives. We may say we are ready for a long-term, committed relationship (that's the flea talking) and be mystified every time yet another relationship blows up in our face (the elephant).

This requires being willing to take an honest look at your life. What is the true state of your relationships, your health, your work, your career?

2. Your own gut sense

Nobody knows yourself better than you do. And even though the conscious mind is unaware of more than 99 percent of what is going on in the subconscious, you are *subconsciously* aware of all of it, 100 percent.

How do you feel as you greet each new day?

3. Feedback from others

While it's true that nobody knows us better than we do ourselves, it is also true that we tend to have blind spots—and sometimes these occur in the areas we most need to see clearly. The people around us, especially those who are close to us, may have the benefit of objectivity.

Just as family members may know of traumatic early events that you have no memory of, there may be family and/or friends who have a truer picture of some of the beliefs that run your life. They may, in other words, more clearly see your elephant than you do.

The Problem with Positive Thinking

Understanding the enormous disparity between the conscious and subconscious functions—the communication gap between flea and elephant, you might say—helps to explain the profound limitations of counseling and other forms of cognitive therapy. When it comes to that persistent and pervasive fog of distress, as we said in the introduction, talking it through just doesn't provide much help.

We have often heard people say, as we explore their history and look at past events that may be causing them distress, "Oh, I already dealt with that in therapy." And indeed, they may have felt better when talking about it and may have even seen some improvements in their lives as a result. Ninety-nine times out of a hundred, though, they have dealt with the issue only on a conscious level—and that is like dealing with the foam on the top of an ocean wave, not the powerful currents deep underneath. It is the subconscious level that really determines the feeling state.

This is why popular approaches to self-improvement, such as positive thinking and affirmations, are so rarely as effective as their adherents hope they will be. Remember, the conscious attention functions something like a penlight in a vast, dark room: it is a powerful little beam, but it can only illuminate the one tiny area where you shine it—and it only illuminates that tiny area while you're shining it there. As soon as you move the beam to light up something else, that first area slips back into darkness. You can put all your heart and soul into consciously thinking, "I deserve love, I deserve love, I deserve love . . ."—and then the moment you go back to your normal routines and are no longer focusing the flashlight of your prefrontal cortex on that thought, your subconscious routines kick in with their one-million-times-more-powerful message: *I am worthless and unlovable.*

The problem with positive thinking is that, while it may be positive, *it's still thinking.* And that is using the power of a flea to divert the path of an elephant.

This is not to say that there is no value in focusing on our conscious awareness. There *are* good conscious techniques that can be quite helpful, which is why cognitive behavioral therapy does have value. When you pay careful attention (conscious awareness) to how you are thinking about things, it can change your emotional state. It's something like learning to play a musical instrument, learning a new language, or learning *anything* new: you have to focus on it consciously at first, practicing it until it starts to become a habit.

The problem is that, when we are dealing with these profoundly ingrained, emotionally charged belief structures that have been seared into our nervous systems by the asteroid strikes of early traumatic experiences, they are tough to change. It is something like bending spring steel: as long as you hold it in that new position, it stays there—but the moment you let go, it springs back to its former shape. In order to effect a genuine and lasting change in these deeply held beliefs, we need to address them at the deepest cellular level.

That is the purpose of step 2, which we'll explore in the next chapter.

Step 1: Identify

Purpose: Identify your strongest self-limiting beliefs.

a. Identify your "asteroid strikes."

- Create a list of past events that you feel may have had a strong negative impact on how you see yourself and your world.

- Go through this list and determine which event seems to you to have had the deepest or most significant impact.

b. Identify your strongest self-limiting beliefs.

- From this checklist of seven self-limiting beliefs, identify which belief feels most pertinent to you:

    I am not safe.

    I am worthless.

    I am powerless.

    I am not lovable.

    I cannot trust anyone.

    I am bad.

    I am alone.

c. Verify the elements you have identified.

- Use neuromuscular feedback to help review both lists and arrive at what you see as the single most pertinent past event and the single most prevalent self-limiting belief.

4

A Disturbance in the Force

I felt a great disturbance in the Force, as if millions of
voices cried out in terror and were suddenly silenced.
—Obi-Wan Kenobi, in *Star Wars*

"WE WERE HIDING IN our church—my family and some other villagers. Suddenly some men came in with machetes. My father turned to me and said, 'Run, Chantal, run—and no matter what happens, don't look back!' "

Chantal was only three years old when the men burst into the church where her family was hiding. She managed to escape—but her father did not. Over the course of that horrific Rwandan summer of 1994, she lost her entire family and every other living soul in her village except herself and one other child. In the years since, her life was beset with flashbacks and nightmares, disrupted sleep, and the whole gamut of classic post-traumatic stress symptoms. Then, in 2006, twelve years after the genocide, a team of researchers came to Rwanda as part of a mission to study a new and unconventional methodology of therapy for post-traumatic stress disorder.

The team's leader, Caroline Sakai, Ph.D., a soft-spoken psychologist from Honolulu, led Chantal through a simple process, having her lightly tap herself on specific points on her skin. As the girl continued tapping, the researcher gently asked her to describe that terrible scene again.

"She started sobbing," recalls Dr. Sakai, "but then, as we started going through the treatment, her tears stopped, and she began to smile. I said, 'What's going on for you right now?' And she said, 'I can remember my father, playing with me.'"

It was a memory she had completely forgotten about up until that moment.

"Fifteen minutes later, she was laughing," reports Dr. Sakai. "She told me how elated she was to have happy memories of her family again." And when Chantal thought back to that terrible scene in the church, she said that, while she could still remember what happened, it was no longer vivid, as if it were still happening *now*. It had faded into the distance, like something from long ago.

After that single session, Chantal's flashbacks and nightmares left her. That night, for the first time in twelve years, she slept.

An Energy Psychology Revolution

Chantal was one of fifty Rwandan orphans who participated in the study. Of the four hundred children in residence at the orphanage, nearly two hundred were survivors of the 1994 slaughter, and among that group the researchers had identified the fifty who rated on a standardized symptom inventory as having the worst post-traumatic stress disorder (PTSD) symptoms. After a single session, forty-seven of the fifty no longer tested in the PTSD range. More remarkably still, when Caroline and her team returned to Rwanda one year later, those results had held. The children's terrible symptoms hadn't just lifted temporarily. They were *gone*.

The landmark study in Rwanda is not an isolated case. Since the early 2000s, there has been a steady stream of studies demonstrating the efficacy of a new model of treatment that has come to be called *energy psychology*.

- One study with traumatized adolescents followed sixteen teen-age boys in Peru who had all been severely abused. Eight received treatment, eight did not. As with the Rwandan orphans, the eight who received the treatment no longer tested in the PTSD range after a single session—and again, those scores held firm at a one-year follow-up.

- In a randomized, double-blind pilot study in South America con-ducted over five and a half years, approximately five thousand pa-tients diagnosed with a range of anxiety disorders were randomly assigned to an experimental group that received energy psychol-ogy treatments, or to a control group that received conventional cognitive behavioral therapy and/or medication. The patients were rated by independent clinicians who did not know which group each patient belonged to, at one-month, three-month, six-month, and one-year intervals. At the close of therapy, 90 percent of the experimental group showed improvement, as opposed to 63 percent of the control group, and 76 percent of the experimen-tal group was judged symptom free, as compared to 51 percent of the control group.

- In a randomized, controlled trial with combat veterans, forty-nine vets showed dramatic improvements after six treatment sessions, and forty-two of the forty-nine—six out of seven—no longer scored above the PTSD cutoff. At a six-month follow-up, these gains had persisted.

To date, there have been studies using these techniques with such diverse conditions as weight loss and long-term weight maintenance, phobias, test anxiety, depression, anxiety, and fibromyalgia, in addi-tion to post-traumatic stress disorder, and there are a slew of others in process, including one study on chronic pain associated with cancer and two additional large-scale studies on post-traumatic stress with veterans at Walter Reed Memorial Hospital and the Columbia Pacific Medical Center in San Francisco.

The work with combat veterans is particularly striking, given the severity of the post-traumatic stress they tend to suffer and the prevalence of the condition. Like the more severe forms of anxiety and depression, severe PTSD is typically considered *treatable but not curable*. But these new studies seem to contradict that conventional wisdom.

For example, one of the therapists in the combat veterans study cited described her work with Keith, an infantry soldier who'd served in the Mekong Delta during the Vietnam War. Keith had seen quite a few casualties on both sides, and now, more than three decades since his tour of duty, he was still tormented with persistent flashbacks. "Sometimes," he told the therapist, "I think I see Viet Cong soldiers hiding behind bushes and trees." The flashbacks, together with intrusive thoughts, an overwhelming sense of guilt, and severe insomnia riddled with nightmares, left him essentially unable to function. Extensive therapy through the Veterans Administration, including both group and individual treatments, had offered no relief.

Keith underwent six one-hour energy psychology sessions with the therapist, during which she had him tap on specific points while he brought his war memories and other stressful experiences to mind. By the end of the six sessions, Keith was getting seven to eight hours of uninterrupted sleep, free of nightmares, and he reported that his other symptoms had abated as well.

A six-month follow-up interview and further testing showed that these improvements had stayed with Keith from that day forward.

Here is what all these remarkable studies share in common: rather than employing medications to treat the *body,* or counseling and behavior modification to treat the *mind*, they all directly address a third aspect of the human organism, one that bridges the gap between mind and body: the *biofield*.

You: A Walking, Talking, Rechargeable Battery

Conventional modern medicine, with its basis in physiology and anatomy and its repertoire of pharmaceuticals, surgery, and other allopathic interventions, fundamentally treats the physical body. Even psychiatric medicine is essentially a physical treatment, addressing symptoms of the mind through the chemical impact of allopathic drugs.

Conventional psychology, on the other hand, fundamentally treats the mind: through talking, behavior modification, and so forth, it seeks to modify how you perceive experiences and think about things, and through this, how you structure your behaviors.

But these two approaches in themselves fail to fully address our new understanding of human health. This new model sees the human being as an organism composed of three aspects: body, mind, and *biofield*—a conductive medium that overlaps and integrates body and mind together.

The scientists and physicians involved with energy work consider the biofield as consisting of at least three principal energy systems:

- The fourteen *meridians* of acupuncture
- The *chakras* or energy centers that form a vertical system running roughly along the spine, typically including seven centers (though some chakra systems count as many as twelve such energy centers)
- The *biofield* itself, a very fine electromagnetic field that begins at the level of the skin and extends outward for several inches or farther

For simplicity's sake, in this book we use the term *biofield* to refer to all of these systems together as one energetic whole.

Perhaps the simplest way to see the biofield, and even demonstrate its existence for yourself, is to look at the body's overall *polarity*.

All electrical and magnetic phenomena exhibit the property of polarity, that is, organization around two poles of opposing electrical charge. This holds true for phenomena on every scale, from the earth itself, to the battery in your cell phone, to a subatomic particle.

It also holds true, as it turns out, for *you*.

During the first half of the twentieth century, the Yale researcher Harold Saxton Burr, Ph.D., discovered something fascinating and fundamental about the biofield: like any other electrical phenomena, all organisms exhibit a north/south electrical polarity. (To read more about Dr. Burr and the fascinating history of biofield research, see Appendix B: Embracing the Biofield.) Measurements taken during surgery with a sensitive galvanometer revealed a distinct pattern of negative and positive electrical charges in individual organs: there was a negative electrical charge on the top of the liver, top of the heart, top of the pancreas, and so forth, and a positive charge at the lower portion of those organs. Likewise, the top of the head, tongue, and palate and upper surface of the hands and feet exhibit a mild negative electrical charge, while the underside of the chin, tongue, and palate and soles of the hands and feet carry a mild positive electrical charge. Even our individual nerve cells are electrically polarized.

Each of us is in essence a human battery with an electrical polarity overall as well as an elaborate arrangement of smaller polarities. Over time Dr. Burr was able to map out this arrangement of electrical polarities of a human being in normal health.

When our physical health or emotional and psychological equilibrium is disrupted, that natural polarity can become disorganized or reversed.

You can easily test your own polarity to see whether it is balanced or reversed using the simple neuromuscular feedback method we learned in chapter 3.

1. Palm to head

Place your hand lightly on top of your head, palm down. It doesn't matter which hand you use. Hold the other arm out to the side and have your tester apply slight downward pressure.

2. Back of hand to head

Now turn your hand over, so that the back of your hand is resting against your head. Have your tester apply downward pressure again.

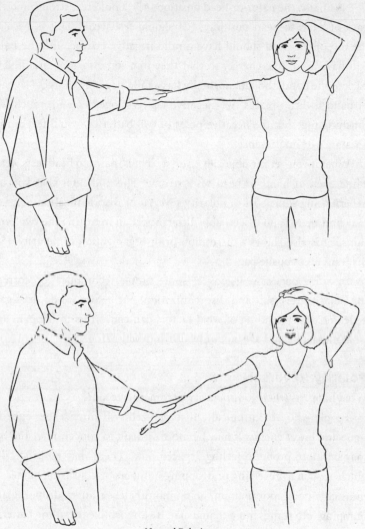

Normal Polarity

Again, remember that the difference between testing strong and testing weak is slight, typically from 5 to 15 percent. This will ordinarily be enough to feel a distinct difference.

Normally, the palm-to-head position (#1) should test strong, and the back-of-hand-to-head position (#2) should test weak. This is because the top of the head should have a mild negative charge, and the palm will have a positive charge, so that they in a sense form a circuit. The back of the hand, though, normally has a mild negative charge—so back of hand to head places two negative charges together and, much like touching together the negative poles of two batteries, you'll feel a mild resistance or interference.

What if you get the opposite results? That is, palm to head tests weak, while back of hand to head tests strong? This indicates that you are experiencing some sort of polarity reversal or disorganization. Or, you may find there is no discernable difference at all in testing the two positions. This also shows a disruption or disorganization of polarity. (See diagram on opposite page.)

In a few pages, we'll look at some simple techniques for correcting polarity reversals and disorganization, but before we do, let's gain a clearer understanding of what factors can cause this to happen, and what impact it can have on our health and well-being.

Polarity Reversals

What happens when your polarity becomes reversed?

People who are chronically disorganized will often experience fatigue and lower energy. It may be more difficult to concentrate, and one may be more prone to feeling "spaced out." There may be processing glitches, such as reversing or dropping numbers or confusing names, or unusually poor coordination, being inordinately clumsy, dropping and bumping into things more than usual. It's almost like installing batteries in a toy car and mistakenly putting them in backward: when you press the GO button, the car goes—but in reverse.

For example, you might feel fine as you sit down to work at your desk, but two hours later realize that you cannot focus, that nothing you're doing is quite working. You may interpret this in all sorts of ways:

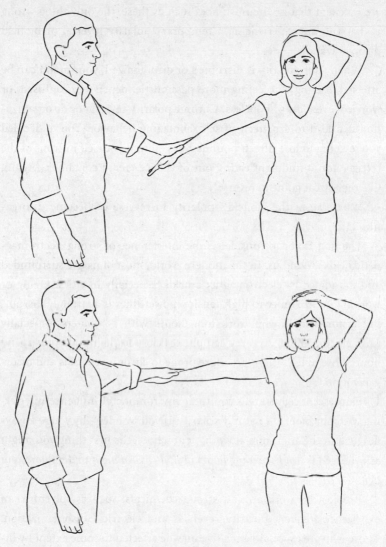

Reversed Polarity

"I just can't think today. I'm not myself today. This problem is too hard. It's writer's block. I'm not up to this challenge. I'm having a bad day." But there is no such thing as a bad day: days are just days. The chances are excellent that in circumstances such as these, the only thing wrong is that you are experiencing a temporary polarity reversal or biofield disorganization.

When your polarity is disrupted or disorganized, your mood can be affected, leaving you feeling more pessimistic, depressed, confused, or worried, even lost or hopeless. Chronic polarity reversal or disorganization can lead to a pattern of self-sabotaging behavior. You've decided you're going to lose fifteen pounds, yet you find yourself in front of the refrigerator at midnight eating out of the ice cream container. (Again, like the toy car going in reverse!)

What causes the biofield's polarity to reverse or become disorganized?

The first factor to consider is the interference of strong electromagnetic fields around us. In the modern world, most of us live surrounded and inundated by electromagnetic fields, especially in cities. Living or working in proximity to high-tension power lines is a strongly disrupting factor. People who work long hours with computers, especially unshielded computers, carry cell phones close to their bodies, or spend hours close to televisions are more prone to chronic reversals and disorganization.

Fluorescent lights are a common environmental influence interfering with our biofield's natural polarity. If you wonder why you're always fatigued in the afternoon at work, or at school, the first thing you might ask yourself is *Am I spending hours in that environment under fluorescent lights?*

People who work around strong chemicals, such as solvents, can experience frequent polarity reversals and electrical disorganization. Those who are especially sensitive may be affected to some extent by ingredients in common household products, such as cleansers, detergents, or shampoos, or by the out-gassing from new carpeting or building materials, especially in brand-new construction. Virtually all of us pump our own gasoline these days, and if we're breathing in vapors or getting the fuel on our hands, it can affect us immediately.

This is not to say that all of these environmental factors *will* disrupt your natural polarity, only that they are possible factors. Not everyone will be disorganized by the same influences, or to the same degree. And it is not generally practical to expect that we can completely eliminate these influences, nor is it necessary. However, simply being aware of factors that can have a strong disruptive influence can help us take whatever steps possible to minimize them.

Then there are human and emotional factors in your environment. Trauma, distress, and strong negative emotions can disrupt your polarity just as readily as a high-tension power line. Even fairly minor disruptions can knock your normal polarity off kilter for the moment. You're cooking and you burn something. You're on a sales call and someone slams the phone down on you. Terrible traffic, a delay at the airport, an argument at work or at home.

For that matter, the stress of other people around us can rub off on us. In much the same way that we can induce a current in a wire by placing it adjacent to another wire that is carrying a current, the electrical disorganization of someone physically near us can bleed onto us, causing electrical disruption and polarity disorganization by induction. Some people experience such chronic reversals that they carry a static cloud with them, much like the character Pig Pen in the old *Peanuts* comic strip. When we say of a person entering the room that he gives us "bad vibes," we may be speaking the literal truth.

When people experience chronic polarity reversals or electrical disorganization, whether caused by toxic chemicals in their work environment, high-tension power lines, a toxic boss or colleague, or a stressful relationship—whatever the cause, chronic reversals can lead to a gradual deterioration of health.

Correcting Your Polarity

The good news is that, as we mentioned in chapter 1, we are beautifully designed to be self-correcting, self-healing organisms. While it is likely that most if not all of us become reversed or disorganized in our polarity from time to time, there is a whole range of human activities we do naturally that turn out to have a polarity-corrective influence.

There are two essential ingredients in any kind of polarity correction:

1. Full, regular, unimpeded breathing, and
2. Crossing your body's midline, in both directions

The cycle of respiration, with its rhythmic alternation of exhale and inhale, is one of the body's fundamental processes for maintaining its electrical organization. Moving or positioning yourself in such a way that you cross the body's midline—such as you do naturally in the left–right coordinated movements of crawling, walking, running, or swimming (especially swimming in the ocean, whose saline water is more electrically conducive to restoring balance than fresh water, let alone chlorinated water)—causes the two hemispheres of the brain to interact and reestablish parity.

If this simple formula—breathe deeply and cross your midline—sounds familiar, it should. You learned a simple example of a polarity corrective in chapter 3: crosshand breathing (see page 94). There, we explained this exercise simply by saying that it would "balance your neuromuscular system." To put it more accurately, it works by reestablishing the biofield's normal electrical polarity.

Let's take another look at this simple exercise from the standpoint of polarity.

- In this and all similar breathing exercises, the deliberate alternation of full inhale and full exhale supports a rhythmic alternation of electrical charge.
- Touching the top of the tongue to the roof of the mouth (on inhale), then touching it to the floor of the mouth (on exhale) helps to reestablish the biofield's electrical organization. Likewise, directing the breath through the nose on inhale, and through the mouth on exhale, helps to reestablish polar organi-

zation, because of the opposite electrical charges at the roof and floor of the mouth cavity.

- Crossing the arms so that the right hand rests on the left side of the body, and vice versa, is an example of what we mean by *crossing the midline*.

This sheds further light on why, in chapter 3, we recommended taking a minute to do crosshand breathing in situations where neuromuscular feedback is giving false readings. In most cases, false readings of simple, objective statements (such as your name, the date, or two plus two equals four) are caused by a reversed or disorganized polarity in either tester or subject. In most cases, a minute or two of crosshand breathing will correct the situation.

There are many ways we do this naturally. For example, when you walk you normally swing your right hand forward together with your left leg, then your left hand together with your right leg, and so forth. This not only creates a physical balance, but also an electrical one.

Later in this chapter we will look at a few additional techniques for correcting polarity, but nine times out of ten, one or two minutes of simple crosshand breathing will do it. We often have clients do a few minutes of crosshand breathing early in the session, and it is remarkable to see how often they experience significant, even dramatic relief simply from this one step.

For example, we recently saw a woman who was experiencing profound difficulties in her health as well as her personal life. After taking a bit of her history, we led her through a couple of minutes of crosshand breathing, just to clear the air so we could continue the session more productively. After a minute, she looked around with a puzzled expression of dawning delight.

"Hey, did it just get brighter in here?" she asked.

We have seen similar responses before—in fact, we have seen it happen thousands of times. Just by correcting their polarity, we often see people transform dramatically. When you start using simple polarity-correctives regularly, it's not unusual to see all sorts of things shift in your life. You don't feel as fatigued, your concentration is sharper, you are less clumsy. It is subtle, but over time, profound. When that light goes on, it can be a life-changing event.

Emptying the Cloud from the Cup

A young truth-seeker visited a wise monk and asked if the old man would tell him the path to peace and perfect joy. The monk invited him to come in and have a cup of tea.

As they sat, the young man began telling his host about his studies, his many years of questing for knowledge, and all that he had learned in his travels. As the truth-seeker talked, the old man just nodded and smiled, nodded and smiled. After a while, as the young man continued to talk, the monk brought out a boiling teapot and two cups. He began pouring tea into the young man's cup and continued pouring, and pouring, and pouring.

Suddenly the young man realized that tea was spilling all over the table and onto the floor. He leaped to his feet and cried out, "Old man, are you nuts?! My cup is already full—it won't take any more tea!"

The monk set the teapot down and looked serenely at his guest—and in that moment the young man became enlightened.

Without uttering a word, the old man had pointed out that his visitor was already so full of his own ideas and thoughts it would have been pointless to tell him anything new about life. Any words the old man might have used would have simply spilled out onto the floor.

This is exactly why the effort to fill ourselves with positive new beliefs, good habits, or resolution to old patterns of thought and behavior are so often frustrated: there is no room for the new beliefs until we empty out the old ones. Again, this explains why such popular approaches as positive thinking and affirmations are so rarely effective in and of themselves. Trying to install a new, positive belief through repeating affirmations, visualizations, mantra-like verbal repetition, vision boards, or even subliminal media, without first clearing out the system's static cloud and its persistent echoes of self-limiting beliefs, is like trying to pour fresh, clean water into a cup that is still full of toxic, brackish water.

As we've explored in the first few chapters of this book, painful events in our past often create a mass of psychological debris, like a cloud of psychic dust kicked up into the atmosphere of our lives. You can think of this as something like an accumulation of static electricity that, unless it is discharged and released, continues to circulate endlessly. This static cloud has both psychological and physiological aspects—that is, it affects us in both mind and body. Yet it is itself neither psychological nor physiological at its core, but *energetic*. It is rooted not fundamentally in mind or body but in our biofield—and if we want to dissipate that fog of distress and bring both mind and body into some sort of functional balance, we need to in some way directly address the biofield.

There are natural ways of discharging this type of disordered electrical charge. Through dreams, for example we can drain away some of that static cloud while we sleep. Various types of exercise and physical activity can help to discharge, mitigate, or soften it to some degree. But if we are going to make a significant transformation and dissipate deeply entrenched patterns of thought and belief that have gnawed at us for years, we need a more focused, more consistent and predictable technique as part of our Four-Step Process.

Mediating Between Flea and Elephant

David Feinstein, Ph.D., who served on the psychiatric staff at Johns Hopkins in the 1970s before becoming intrigued with the emerging field of energy psychology, says an ongoing study at Harvard using brain imaging to observe in real time the effects on the brain of acupuncture may illuminate the mechanism behind the extraordinary success rates of studies like Caroline Sakai's Rwandan experience. Explains Dr. Feinstein:

What the Harvard studies have shown, is that when you stimulate certain acupressure points, this sends a signal to the amygdala that decreases arousal. This explains a lot, in terms of how energy psychology works.

When you have a conditioned response to a certain memory—say, jealousy, or anger, or fear—bringing up that memory increases arousal in the amygdala. But when you activate the correct acupressure point at the same time that you are bringing up that memory, then you are simultaneously sending a signal to *decrease* arousal. When you send this deactivating signal several times, it becomes the new normal. You literally change the response associated with that memory.

Bringing the memory to mind stimulates the amygdala, provoking the stress response. But stimulating the acupoint at the same time sends an opposite calming or sedating impulse. In effect, you are retraining the amygdala and its associated pathways to interpret the memory differently. By addressing the biofield directly, in other words, you completely bypass the cognitive process and recondition the subconscious neural response. Dr. Feinstein calls this process *acupressure-assisted exposure therapy.*

Remember what happened with Chantal? Dr. Sakai had her bring the traumatic memory of her family's murder to mind while she was tapping acupoints. In other words, this exactly followed Dr. Feinstein's description. Her amygdala was being given two different messages: the memory was stimulating the trauma response, but the touching of the acupoints sent an opposite, calming message.

Here is the fascinating thing about this sequence. Bringing a memory to mind is a conscious act of cognition (the flea). However, the amygdala and its associated neural pathways are domains of the subconscious (the elephant). What Dr. Feinstein is describing is a process of mediating between the conscious and subconscious faculties—flea and elephant—*by directly addressing the biofield.*

"This is not something you can simply will yourself to do," as Dr. Feinstein puts it, "because it is a physiological response, based on neural pathways that you built during the traumatic event."

This sequence is reflected precisely in the first two steps of our Four-Step Process.

In step 1, you identify the specific painful memory or past experience that most closely connects to the stressed state of mind you want to release, as well as the specific negative, self-limiting belief associated with that memory. Then, with those cognitive elements freshly in mind, you engage step 2 to clear, disentangle, and dissipate them.

Step 2

Before we can dissolve and eliminate those negative patterns and replace them with the new, positive ones we want to have, we need to clear out the static cloud from our biofield. That is the essential purpose of step 2.

For the past several decades, we have used a broad inventory of tools and methodologies in our practice, including methods such as eye movement desensitization and reprocessing (EMDR) and the acupoint tapping used by Caroline Sakai in Rwanda. For the Four-Step Process, though, we wanted to use something simpler. The approach you are learning right now is a distillation of many methodologies, boiled down to its essence to produce a protocol that is both effective and practical.

Step 2 consists of two simple exercises: crosshand breathing, and grounding.

Crosshand Breathing

This exercise typically corrects a disorganized or reversed polarity. Even if one's polarity is not reversed, crosshand breathing will help to clear that static buzz, to rebalance and sharpen the biofield. Clients commonly experience a sense of lightness, clarity, and heightened mood simply from one or two minutes of crosshand breathing. In addition to its role in the Four-Step Process, it is something you can practice on its own, simply and quickly, virtually anytime and anywhere.

Although we went through this in chapter 3, we'll walk you through it again here:

- In a seated position, cross your left ankle over your right.
- Place your left hand across your chest, so that the fingers rest over the right side of your collarbone. Then cross your right hand over your left, so that the fingers of your right hand rest over the left side of your collarbone.
- Breathe in through your nose and out through your mouth. As you breathe in, let your tongue touch the roof of your mouth, just behind your front teeth. As you breathe out again, let your tongue rest behind your lower front teeth. You may close your eyes or look down toward the floor to reduce visual stimuli.

Grounding

After about two minutes of crosshand breathing, then do the following exercise to stabilize and ground your biofield:

- Sit straight and relaxed. Place both hands, one on top of the other, over your solar plexus, just below the bottom of your rib cage. Feel your breath in your belly, slowly rising and falling.
- Now close your eyes, and visualize a cable extending downward from your body straight into the earth.
- Hold that image, breathing slowly in and out, for about one minute.

The grounding exercise is analogous to the grounding of an electrical appliance. It also conveys to the subconscious a sense of being firmly rooted—in reality, in one's identity, in the truth of your own strengths and abilities.

Optional Methods

The combination of crosshand breathing for two minutes, followed by a minute of grounding, is a powerful step 2 and sufficient to correct the biofield's polarity nine times out of ten.) However, there are several alternative exercises for polarity correction that can be useful in extreme cases or in times of greater than normal stress.

Cross Crawl

Sometimes crosshand breathing alone does not correct a person's polarity. You can assess whether this is the case for you simply by using neuromuscular feedback, as we described earlier: palm on top of head versus back of hand on top of head.

In cases in which crosshand breathing alone does not correct a polarity reversal, we often use a simple exercise we call *cross crawl*.

- In a standing position, lift your left knee up to waist-high position and slap it gently with your right hand.
- Then do the opposite, lifting your right knee and slapping it with your left hand.
- Continue alternating, gently slapping each knee with the opposite hand, in an easy walking rhythm. Take care to breathe normally as you do this. Continue for about two minutes.

This seems like a fairly simple, straightforward task. Surprisingly, though, it is not always as easy as it looks, especially at first.

You've heard the expression, "You have to crawl before you can walk." There is much truth to this. In fact, there is significant neurological development that occurs in infants that is supported by the act of learning to crawl. The complex movement sequence, with its left–right integration, has an impact on the left–right integration of the brain's hemispheres, and there is evidence that in infants in whom the crawling stage is impeded, held back, or skipped over, there are negative neurological consequences.

It's interesting to note that in cases where crosshand breathing alone does not restore normal electrical polarity, the person may at first have a difficult time getting the hang of the cross crawl. In people who have chronic polarity reversals, there is often a sense of clumsiness or awkward coordination. We have often seen clients have to work at the cross crawl for a minute or two before suddenly catching it—and then all at once, they can not only do it but do it smoothly and easily, even talking at the same time. You can literally see the reorganization of their polarity unfolding in real time. ⌐

The Diamond Gait

As we said earlier, such normal activities as walking, running, or swimming embody the basic components of polarity correction: full breathing and a rhythmic crossing of the midline. Sometimes even a short walk can unblock us. Writers and other creative artists throughout history have described this: after even a fairly short, brisk walk, it's almost as if you can hear the tumblers falling into place.

John Diamond, M.D., one of the great pioneers of neuromuscular feedback, recommended a slightly exaggerated walking as a simple polarity corrective, which he termed the *Diamond gait*.

The key to the Diamond gait is to walk at a brisk pace and accentuate the swing of your arms so that they fully cross the body midline. In other words, the right arm swings forward and across the body, well toward the left, followed by the left arm swinging forward and well toward the right.

Using this exercise to fully correct a polarity reversal will typically take a brisk walk of at least ten minutes.

Alternate Nostril Breathing

Alternate nostril breathing is well known to practitioners of yoga, where it holds a central place and is often refined to an elaborate science. If you are experiencing persistent or chronic polarity reversals, practicing a simple version of this structured right–left breathing pattern several times a day can serve as an "extra strength" corrective:

- Place your right thumb against your right nostril, closing it. Inhale through your left nostril.

- Release your thumb and press your index finger against your left nostril, closing it. Now exhale through your right nostril.
- Continue this alternating pattern, inhaling through your left nostril and exhaling through your right, ten times.
- Now reverse the process, this time using the thumb and forefinger of your *left* hand, inhaling through the right nostril and exhaling through the left. Repeat this ten times.

This entire exercise, ten times in one direction and ten times in the other, should take a total of about two or three minutes.

This can feel a little complicated, especially when one is already electrically disorganized. The more you practice it, the more natural it begins to feel.

Spill or Stain?

Not every painful experience leaves a lasting mark. There are upsets that can be soothed and settled by the balm of time, hurt feelings that yield to the comfort of a good cry, doubts and fears that can be assuaged by a sympathetic ear. Likewise, there are improvements in ourselves, shifts in our state of mind, and steps forward in our maturation as human beings that we can readily make sheerly through our conscious will. Sometimes, affirmations and positive thinking really *do* work.

But then there are changes we simply cannot make through the unaided effort of our good intentions.

Some emotional events are like spills—they are messy, but not that difficult to mop up. So you were teased in school? Scolded by your parents, yelled at by a coach, went through a painful breakup in high school? Yes, it hurt, but nine times out of ten, it's nothing you can't wipe up with a little soap, hot water, and paper towels.

Some events, though, are more than spills. They are *stains*, and no amount of scrubbing can get them out.

If you have a deeply rooted belief, based on past microtrauma patterning, that you cannot be successful, then you may be able to shift that through a focused effort of your will and intention . . . for the moment. But if you have not first cleared out the underlying negative beliefs and other interference patterns deeply ingrained in your subconscious, the old belief will inevitably reassert itself.

However, if you *do* first clear away the old debris and lay a foundation for your new belief, then it will be able to install itself for the long haul. When you properly clear a stress that is encoded in past memory, it's done: it's *gone*. Just as happened for Chantal, the Rwandan survivor, and for Keith, the Vietnam vet, the past memories remain, but they lose their sting and power.

At which point you are ready to install a set of new, positive beliefs—and that is what chapter 5 is all about.

Step 2: Clear

*Purpose: Rebalance your body's energy
system and prepare it for repatterning.*

a. Crosshand breathing (two minutes)

- In a seated position, cross your left ankle over your right.

- Place your left hand across your chest, so that the fingers rest over the right side of your collarbone. Then cross your right hand over your left, so that the fingers of your right hand rest over the left side of your collarbone.

- Breathe in through your nose and out through your mouth. As you breathe in, let your tongue touch the roof of your mouth, just behind your front teeth. As you breathe out again, let your tongue rest behind your lower front teeth. You may close your eyes or look down toward the floor to reduce visual stimuli.

b. Grounding (one minute)

- Sit straight and relaxed. Place both hands, one on top of the other, over your solar plexus, just below the bottom of your rib cage. Feel your breath in your belly, slowly rising and falling.

- Now close your eyes, and visualize a cable extending down from your body straight down into the earth.

- Hold that image, breathing slowly in and out, for about one minute.

c. Optional methods

- Use neuromuscular feedback to check your biofield's polarity.

- For persistent or chronic reversal or disorganization, you may also use:

   Cross crawl: about two minutes

   Diamond gait: at least ten minutes

   Alternate nostril breathing: ten cycles in both directions, about two or three minutes

CHAPTER FIVE

Your Personal Code to Joy

I think I can, I think I can . . .
—The Little Engine That Could

"I'M NOT SURE I really see any point in trying." The woman in our office sat slumped in her chair, listless and defeated. "They're saying I won't live to see my next birthday. So what sort of goals should I be looking to achieve here?"

A retired dental hygienist, Lydia was in her mid-sixties, what these days is considered a relatively young age. By rights, she ought to have decades of life to look forward to. However, about a year earlier, she had been diagnosed with brain cancer. Despite surgery and radiation, her prognosis was not good. Not surprisingly, Lydia had become quite depressed, and this was the reason her internist and oncologist had referred her to us.

As we took her history, we learned that Lydia had been plagued by a number of issues in her life, including a difficult upbringing with a father who was extremely overbearing and even mean. As an adult, she married someone who followed in a pattern of behavior quite similar to her father's. The marriage ended in a bitter divorce. Then came the cancer.

Lydia's hair had all fallen out during treatment. Now it was starting to come in again, and in that first visit, she confided to us that she hated how it looked. We thought it looked fantastic and told her so. But she didn't believe us. She also mentioned in the next breath that she did not especially like the way her voice sounded. She had a beautiful voice, we told her, and she had beautiful hair. We weren't just saying these things because we wanted her to feel good. They were the absolute truth. Lydia is a lovely person, and it showed. But, at this point in her life, she was fundamentally incapable of accepting herself.

We walked her through the four steps of the process, focusing on the deep beliefs she had formed early on as a result of her father's constant carping. She began to feel a shift, but the change was not dramatic (at least not right away), and we scheduled additional visits to help her work through the layers of issues. As we continued meeting and she continued working with the steps of the process, she gradually began to blossom.

When she came to see us that first time, there was a note in her medical file saying that she had been referred to us for "treatment for anxiety and depression." A few visits later, we noticed a new notation in the file: "Depression and anxiety resolved."

Resolved—that's not a word you will very often see doctors associate with the phrase *anxiety and depression*. But it was not her mood alone that was resolved. Everything about Lydia began to shift from that point on. Even her physical health began to improve. Before long, she was vibrant and full of life—and her tumors began to shrink. Her doctors were frankly baffled, but they couldn't deny the reality of what was happening before their eyes. Her prognosis changed. There were birthdays once again in Lydia's future.

What happened here? The shift that Lydia made occurred on several levels at once. In becoming consciously aware of her self-limiting beliefs, together with some of the early experiences that had fueled them, she made a cognitive shift—but by clearing out the static cloud of debris in her biofield, she was also able to bring that shift deep into the level of her subconscious mind. And once that fog of distress lifted, it was possible for her to starting holding a different image of herself.

In a sense, Lydia became healthy because she became able to *see herself* as healthy.

Images: Language of the Subconscious

This power of images to model and mold our reality is central to the Four-Step Process. If the subconscious is the elephant that shapes and drives our actions, choices, and, to a great extent, our destiny, images are the way to communicate with that elephant. Images are the language of the subconscious.

Human beings have a very special ability: we are able to create inside our brains a realistic model of external events and to an extraordinary degree use that internal model in turn to influence and drive the outcome of external events.

In a sense, it is this ability to create powerful mental images of external realities that made possible the development of human civilization itself, as our colleague V. S. Ramachandran, M.D., Ph.D., points out in his wonderful book, *The Tell-Tale Brain*. This natural imaging capacity, says Dr. Ramachandran, is embodied in what have been colorfully dubbed "mirror neurons," neural circuits that are activated when we observe the actions of others and replicate their neurological underpinnings inside our own brains, as if we were performing the actions ourselves.

"It is as if mirror neurons are nature's own virtual reality simulations of the intentions of other beings," says Dr. Ramachandran.

The new understanding of mirror neurons helps to explain an entire body of research, going back for more than a hundred years, that says the images we hold in our minds can have a tangible impact on our behavior and physical abilities.

Many of these studies have focused on the ability of "mental rehearsal" to improve athletic performance. For example, in one oft-cited

1977 study, a group of seventy-two college basketball players was split into four groups, all of whom went through a series of fifteen practice sessions on the court over a six-week period. The sessions were identical in every way except that, just prior to practice, three of the four groups were taken through ten minutes of preparation. Players in the first group were put through five minutes of relaxation followed by five minutes of guided visualization in which they imagined themselves throwing baskets from the free throw line. During those five-minute sessions, they were told to recall the sensory impressions of being on the court.

"Try to feel your sensations at the moment you approach the foul line," the voice on the tape told the players as they sat, eyes closed, listening carefully. "Possibly you can feel your heart pounding. Your legs may feel tired, shaky, or weak. Sweat may be rolling down your back or neck. You may notice the crowd has become more quiet; you may even be able to feel their eyes on you. Take a moment and feel your sensations as you approach the foul line. . . ." The players concluded each session by visualizing themselves making perfect shots.

The second group received five minutes of relaxation only, together with another five minutes of a bogus concentration exercise inserted purely to control for time (that is, so that groups A, B, and C would each have a full ten minutes of preparation time). The third group got the five minutes of visualization together with the bogus concentration exercise. The fourth group got no special preparation at all, only their normal practice session of repetitive drills and free throw practice.

After the six-week training period, all four groups were put through their paces on the court. The first group, consisting of the players who had practiced both relaxation and visualization, showed a statistically significant improvement in their performance; the second and third groups had both *slightly* improved. The fourth group had not improved at all. Similar results were found in subsequent studies employing a similar visualization process in such fields as karate, tennis serving, and pistol marksmanship.

With the evidence of newer brain-imaging methods, scientists have now been able to observe what is happening in such experiments: when a subject *imagines* doing something, the exact same areas and pathways in the brain are activated as when actually *doing* it.

"One reason we can change our brains simply by imagining," says Norman Doidge, M.D., in *The Brain That Changes Itself*, "is that, from a neuroscientific point of view, imagining an act and doing it are not as different as they sound." And this is not a purely mental phenomenon: these vivid images can have real, physical consequences.

Dr. Doidge describes an extraordinary experiment conducted in the early 1990s by Drs. Guang Yue and Kelly Cole. The study looked at two groups, one who performed a set of specific physical exercises and one who only imagined doing those same exercises. Both groups continued this five days a week for four weeks. At the end of the study, the group who had physically performed the exercises had increased the strength of the muscles involved by 30 percent, while the other group—those who had practiced the identical exercises *only in their imagination*—had strengthened those same muscles by 22 percent.

In other words, simply by imagining they were doing the exercises, the second group physically strengthened the relevant muscles more than two-thirds as much as did the group who actually did the exercises.

Changing Our Genes

If mental rehearsal can strengthen our muscles and improve our score at hoops, might it do something even more dramatic? Such as, say, improve our physical health, even help us recover from an illness? Evidently so, and Lydia is not the first person to have this experience. As with athletics, there is a considerable body of evidence linking positive imagery to physiological health.

Probably the most well-known case is that of the essayist and *Saturday Review* editor Norman Cousins, whose triumph over a life-threatening collagen disease through the power of laughter and positive imagery (along with hearty doses of vitamin C) was chronicled in his 1979 book *Anatomy of an Illness as Perceived by the Patient*. Cousins's book offered a dramatic illustration of the impact thoughts and feelings can have on human health, and it did much to help this idea begin making its way into mainstream Western thought.

What made Cousins's case especially compelling was that he recovered from a life-threatening illness by focusing on his emotions and mental images, not once, but *twice*. In 1980, a decade and a half after the publication of *Anatomy of an Illness*, Cousins suffered a heart attack that nearly killed him. Determined to once again take his life in his own hands and mind, he embarked on another regimen of self-healing and subsequently described his self-recovery program in his 1983 book *The Healing Heart*.

"The life-force may be the least understood force on earth," wrote Cousins. "William James said that human beings tend to live too far within self-imposed limits. It is possible that these limits will recede when we respect more fully the natural drive of the human mind and body toward perfectibility and regeneration. Protecting and cherishing that natural drive may well represent the finest exercise of human freedom."

Our colleague Bruce Lipton, Ph.D., is a pioneer in the field of *epigenetics*, the study of the factors that influence our genes. According to Dr. Lipton's research, our genes don't just suddenly turn on or turn off because they are programmed by some hereditary force over which we have no control. In fact, our genes are influenced by their environment, including the biochemistry of the bloodstream, which is profoundly influenced by our thoughts and emotions.

When we change our beliefs, as Dr. Lipton explains in his landmark book *The Biology of Belief*, we change our biochemistry, at least to some extent, which in turn has an impact on our genes. In other words, change your beliefs, and you change the health, behavior, and fate of your cells.

"Positive thoughts have a profound effect on behavior and genes . . . ," writes Dr. Lipton, "and negative thoughts have an equally powerful effect. When we recognize how these positive and negative beliefs control our biology, we can use this knowledge to create lives filled with health and happiness." 〉

Stepping into Your Own Shoes

Another key to understanding what happened to Lydia (and to Norman Cousins) is the concept of *executive function*, which means the capacity to take control of the circumstances and direction of your own life. In psychology, this is called *self-efficacy*.

The concept and importance of self-efficacy were championed starting in the 1970s by the noted Canadian psychologist Albert Bandura, one of the most influential psychologists of the twentieth century. According to Dr. Bandura, *self-efficacy* refers to our beliefs about our ability to "exercise influence over events that affect [our] lives." In other words, it means acting with the knowledge that you are in the driver's seat of your life. Having self-efficacy means, in essence, stepping into your own shoes.

This is one of the central concepts underlying the Four-Step Process.

When you have self-efficacy, it means the source and center of control in your life is internal, not external. Misfortunes and other external influences cannot completely throw you, because you see yourself as being at the *cause* rather than at the *effect* of circumstances. You cannot always "fix" the circumstance or solve the external problem, but you can always shift how you perceive it. In other words, even if you cannot always solve the problem, you can always solve the dilemma.

This is not to say one should ignore external circumstances. Clearly, it is important to maintain a healthy sense of external reality. But having strong self-efficacy means that the primary source of our validation comes from within, not from without. The praise of others, the diplomas and accolades, the approval and kudos, even the love of those close to you, these are all external validation. If your sense of self is dependent on such external sources, then you are prone to suffering at the mercy of circumstance.

People with poor self-efficacy, says Bandura, constantly doubt their own capabilities:

[Those with poor self-efficacy] shy away from difficult tasks, which they view as personal threats. They have low aspirations and weak commitment to the goals they choose to pursue. When faced with difficult tasks, they dwell on their personal deficiencies, on the obstacles they will encounter, and all kinds of adverse outcomes rather than concentrate on how to perform successfully. They slacken their efforts and give up quickly in the face of difficulties. . . . It does not require much failure for them to lose faith in their capabilities. They fall easy victim to stress and depression.

By contrast, here is his description of people with strong self-efficacy:

People with high assurance in their capabilities approach difficult tasks as challenges to be mastered rather than as threats to be avoided. . . . They set themselves challenging goals and maintain strong commitment to them. They heighten and sustain their efforts in the face of failure. They quickly recover their sense of efficacy after failures or setbacks . . . [and] approach threatening situations with assurance that they can exercise control over them. Such an efficacious outlook produces personal accomplishments, reduces stress, and lowers vulnerability to depression.

Sharon, in her mid-thirties, was a field agent with the FBI. A year or two before she came to see us, Sharon had fallen in love with Harry, another agent, while they were working on a case together. Despite strict FBI policy discouraging fraternization among the agents, the two quietly began living together. However, Sharon soon realized that Harry wasn't ready to commit for the long term. Heartbroken, she nevertheless knew the relationship had to end, and she broke it off.

More than a year passed, and just as Sharon was beginning to feel she was over the breakup, she and Harry were assigned to a training program that would have them working together daily for the next six months. Sharon was in a bind: she feared this would be an intolerable situation, yet she couldn't explain her dilemma to her superiors, because the relationship was never supposed to have happened in the first place.

As the training began, Sharon found herself going through such turmoil that she could barely function. She came home each day miserable, her stomach in knots, often in tears. A friend, seeing how she was suffering, referred her to our office.

As Sharon went through the Four-Step Process, she discovered that her beliefs about men included the classic image of being saved by a knight on a white horse. Without realizing it consciously, she had been carrying this image for many years, along with the belief it fostered, which said, "I cannot take care of myself—I need someone to take care of me."

It was this image, together with all it represented, that lay at the core of Sharon's present anguish. She had given up her sense of control over her own destiny to this image of the man on the horse and thus completely undermined her own self-efficacy.

Once she identified that unsupportive belief, she was able to access her own resources and take care of herself, both practically and emotionally. She stepped into her own shoes and reclaimed her self-efficacy—and was able to go through the remaining five months of training with ease and composure.

Self-efficacy is not a black-and-white, all-or-nothing proposition. Most of us feel a degree of self-efficacy in some or even many areas of our lives, yet we may lack it in others. We may be doing well in our work life, but not in our family life, or vice versa. We may be high-functioning individuals in general, but have certain areas where we feel incompetent or out of our depth, like David, the high-functioning but directionally challenged journalist.

Sharon was completely capable in her work as a law enforcement agent. In fact, the nature of her work required an unusually strong ability to think fast and be powerfully in control of circumstances—and Sharon was good at what she did. It was only when she stepped into the realm of personal relationships that the self-limiting beliefs instilled during childhood would rear their ugly heads and tell her, "You can't do anything right."

Likewise, Lydia was doing fine in her life until she retired from her work as a dental hygienist, because in her work and career, her sense of self-efficacy was intact, and this served as a kind of anchor in her life. Once she was retired and no longer exercising her executive function in that professional capacity, circumstances began getting the upper hand.

What we need, in order to let go of our past self-limiting beliefs and live our ideal life, is to step into a full sense of executive function in our life as a whole—to step fully into our own shoes.

As it turns out, this is something we have been striving to do from the day we were born.

The Road to Becoming You

As a newborn infant, you marveled at this world of sights and sounds. You cooed and gurgled, reached out and touched, putting everything you could manage to manipulate into your mouth as a primal way of connecting with it and learning more about it. Soon you were pushing your explorations further as you crawled, stood, and walked. You were absorbing new observations a mile a minute in what was without question the most accelerated period of learning in your life.

However, in everything you learned, there was one thing you did not yet grasp: that there was such a thing as *you*.

Then, typically at around the age of two, something happened. Ask any parent, and they'll know what it was: you started saying, "No!" Asked to do something, you declined, and not politely. Seeing another child with a toy, you would point (or grab) and declaim, "Mine!" You found an infinite variety of creative ways to refuse, declare, and insist.

Not every child exhibits this behavior at exactly the age of two, and not everyone manifests it the same way, but we all pretty much go through this phase. In fact, it's a critically important stage of development. It is not about negation. It is about assertion.

This is when we learn to distinguish between this thing called "me" and everything else. We develop an awareness of ourselves as autonomous, self-determining beings. It is the beginning of our establishing an individual identity, together with our capacity to negotiate our existence in the world. It is the beginning of what in adulthood will become our fully formed executive function.

To a great extent, this outward journey is also a reflection of what is happening physically in the development of our brain and nervous system, especially in relation to a rich, fatty substance called *myelin*.

Myelin is the material our bodies produce to coat our nerve fibers, forming a fatty sheath that insulates the nerves and, much like the rubber or plastic insulation on household electrical wires, prevents their electrical impulses from short-circuiting or spilling out into their surroundings. This insulation focuses the nerves' capacity to transmit impulses and allows them to transmit as much as one hundred times faster—something like upgrading one's Internet connection from dial-up to broadband.

Very little myelin exists in the brain at the time of birth. As the nervous system begins to myelinate (that is, to form that insulating myelin sheath around the nerves), it starts with the spinal cord and most primitive structures of the brain, proceeding quite gradually to the parts of the brain responsible for higher functions, with the areas of the most sophisticated mental processing in the cerebral cortex coming last of all.

In the first few years of life, in other words, the brain is still largely unmyelinated—still working on a dial-up connection, so to speak. The frontal cortex does not develop sufficiently to have any significant degree of executive function until the age of nine or ten, and even then, the process is nowhere near complete.

Up until the late 1990s, it was believed that the myelination process was complete by age eighteen. However, more recent research has revealed that this doesn't happen fully until well into our twenties. In other words, up until our middle or late twenties, we don't really have the physiological foundation for a fully developed sense of executive function.

Our Hypnotic Childhood

As adults, we can step outside a situation and look at it objectively. We can consider what might be motivating the other people involved as well as how the situation might be affecting them. This level of abstraction gives us a tremendous capacity to process and understand events—a capacity we do not have as children.

When we are very young, everything that happens around us and to us is all about *us*. We don't yet have that capacity of abstraction until the age of nine or ten, and even then not nearly as fully as we will past the age of twenty.

We mentioned earlier that we typically do not clearly remember things that occurred to us when we were two or three years old. But why should this be true? After all, these events certainly had as much impact as later events. If we can clearly remember events that happened five years ago, ten or twenty years ago, why not events when we were two?

In large part, this is because our brains were not sufficiently developed to process these events with the adult skills of executive function and self-efficacy. We did not have the language skills or conceptual objectivity in place to put words and reason to these events when they were happening. Today, as grown adults, we process most of what happens to us in articulated, verbal terms. But when we try to zero in on these events of early childhood, it's very difficult to do. We literally do not have the words to bring them up, because we never attached words to them in the first place. We remember them only in nonverbal, indistinct masses of feeling and emotion.

Lack of executive function means we cannot *observe* the situation, cannot step back and see it objectively. We lack the ability to differentiate what is real from what is not. We have no filters. We simply soak it all up like a sponge.

In psychological terms, we go through those early years in a *hypnagogic* state, meaning that state between full wakefulness and sleep when we are partially conscious but deeply suggestive—when the doorways to our subconscious are wide open.

In a very real sense, we go through our early childhood in something very much like an eyes-open form of hypnotic trance. Whatever your parents or other adults tell you, you tend to accept as true. If your father says, "You are amazing, you can do whatever you set out to do," then as far as you're concerned, that's the truth. Unfortunately, it also works the other way: if he says, "You're worthless, you're good for nothing," then *that* becomes the truth for you.

Again, this is not a verbal concept: it's not as if you say in your mind, "I, Caitlyn, am a worthless human being." No, you don't have any idea what the word *worthless* means, at least not intellectually. Your cerebral cortex doesn't have the myelination or the verbal skills to put that together. Because you don't place words to what you're experiencing, you don't have a verbally articulated memory connected to it. But emotionally, you get the full impact of the message: *I'm not okay. There's something wrong with me.* And that belief is so powerful that years later, in your adult life, despite your accomplishments and all the rest of the evidence that this is not true, you still have the belief locked firmly in place.

According to Bessel van der Kolk, M.D., trauma has a particular impact on the *posterior cingulate*, which is the part of the brain where we assemble our internal perception of ourselves—in technical terms, it is the *enteroceptive* portion of the brain. People who are traumatized, explains Dr. van der Kolk, have more difficulty with self-awareness because the neural site of their sense of self has literally been damaged.

When trauma remains untreated, it can over time profoundly suppress our sense of self-reflection and self-examination.

By the same token, he adds, by healing trauma one can actually grow and deepen that self-reflective part of the brain.

Your Perfect Childhood

Imagine you were raised by the perfect parents—people who completely supported you, championed you, praised you at every accomplishment and encouraged you at every setback, and were always in your corner. Imagine what it would be like to be a kid with parents who are always telling you how great you are, how much potential you have, how much they believe in you, how you can do whatever you set your mind to, how if you follow your heart and pursue the life you truly want you will overcome all obstacles and absolutely cannot fail.

Of course, that's probably not exactly what happened. Your parents may have been wonderful. But no parent is perfect, however well intentioned. We are all human beings, and as parents, we are bound to have "off" days, suffer from our own stresses, and make mistakes. Many of our parenting missteps are probably minor and easily overridden, but there are bound to be some that have significant and lasting impact.

And then, when we were kids, there were also the friends and playmates, the other kids in school, the teachers and coaches, neighborhood parents, and all the other influences in our lives. The teasing, scolding, arguments, unfairnesses, and other emotional scrapes and pains of growing up.

No, you probably did not have the perfect childhood. But what if you had?

Imagine if you *had* had those perfect parents, and together with them, nothing but the most supportive friends and only the best teachers. How you would have turned out? What would your life look and feel like today if you had been nurtured and developed in such a way that you had an absolutely unshakable sense of belief in yourself and the fundamental goodness of the world around you?

Well, that is exactly the life you *can* live—because that is exactly what the Four-Step Process does. It has the impact on your core being that those perfect parents would have had over the years—only you do it yourself. When you go through the steps of this process, you take the beliefs you consciously want running your life and install them into your being at that same preverbal, prearticulate level where you experienced your original learning as an infant. You bypass all the structures and limitations of intellect and verbal, cognitive thought, and imprint your new intentions at a very primal level.

The Four-Step Process is in essence the equivalent of giving yourself a perfect childhood. You are replicating a primal dynamic, invoking the same basic process but doing it in a more structured and much more rapid way.

That is what the Four-Step Process is for. It is a tool to help you complete the process of becoming you.

Step 3

Step 3 brings together elements from everything we've looked at up to this point. It uses the cognitive powers of the conscious mind and the powerful forces of the subconscious, incorporates exercises that help to reorganize your electrical polarity and directly address the biofield, and brings it all together with some powerful images.

There are three parts to this step:

1. Create an image of a *healing basket* and use it to remove from your life any elements of distress.
2. Create a *pledge of self-acceptance* and combine it with a new *self-empowering belief* to form your own *personal code to joy*.
3. Flesh these statements out and make them real to your subconscious using a collection of *scenes from your ideal life*.

Creating a Healing Basket

Picture in your mind's eye a container. We call this a "healing basket," but it can be any kind of container. If you like, you can visualize a bucket, a bowl, or a deep well. "Basket" is simply a metaphor—the concept is *containment*.

Into this container you are going to place the issues and problems you want to let go of, including any self-limiting beliefs and memories of past negative events, as well as any negative factors in your present life that you want to change. The point of the healing basket is that you are exercising your executive power to define and control the situation, and you are using this capacity to contain the pain, struggle, hurt, or challenges that have held you back up until now.

The image of the basket (or whatever container you decide on) is a signal to your subconscious mind that you are in the driver's seat of your life and that the disturbances and issues you are addressing are going to be contained. They are not going to leak out into your life anymore. You are creating a boundary.

Sometimes clients ask us, "How do I know if I'm doing this right? What if I'm not a visual person?" Don't worry. There is no wrong way here, and you don't have to be a visual artist to do this. We've had people tell us, "I'm not good at visualizing things." Fine, we say. Close your eyes for a moment—now, can you imagine the outline of an apple? Sure you can. How did you do that? You visualized it. Anyone can do this.

- Close your eyes and picture your healing basket.
- Place into it all the elements of your fog of distress.

Place into the healing basket the negative, self-limiting beliefs and any other negative elements you identified in step 1, all the hurt, the struggles, the painful memories and past events.

If anything else negative occurs to you while you're doing this, even if it's not something you thought about before when you were going through step 1, toss it in there. Don't worry about it overflowing.

It's your basket: it can hold as much as you need it to. Whatever isn't working in your life, whatever makes you feel overwhelmed, whatever thoughts, feelings, or hardships interfere with your present life, and going back as far as you can remember—throw it all in there.

- Now, over the next two or three minutes, visualize that healing basket slowly disappearing or drifting away.

A simple way to do this is to imagine placing the basket onto the water's surface at the edge of a lake or ocean, and then watching it gradually float away and disappear over the horizon. Or, you might imagine tying a balloon to its handle and watch it gradually drift up and into the clouds.

We have had clients imagine their healing basket as a rocket ship that blasted off into space; as a giant toilet that flushed; as a Dumpster that was picked up and carried away by a trash truck; as a mountain cave that was swallowed up in an earthquake. It doesn't matter exactly what imagery you use. What matters is that you clearly decide on an image that you can focus on, and that the image includes these two crucial ingredients: *containment* and *release*.

If nothing else strongly comes to mind, the default image we recommend is a large straw basket that you place onto the water's surface at the ocean's edge, and gradually watch it carried away, into and over the horizon.

There is a fascinating concept in psychology called the *Zeigarnik principle*, after the Russian psychologist Bluma Zeigarnik, who discovered in the 1920s that people have a better recall of incomplete objects and tasks than of complete ones. For example, waiters remember a meal only as long as the order is still in the process of preparation. Once the meal is served, the order vanishes from the waiter's short-term (that is, conscious) memory. Simply stated, the Zeigarnik principle says.

We remember that which is unfinished or incomplete.

To put it the other way, once a task or issue *is* complete, it then—and *only* then—disappears from view. We worry about things in which we have not achieved closure. Unresolved issues in your life sit around in your psyche like unanswered emails in your psychological and energetic in-box. After you answer the emails, though—*zip!*—they immediately flush out of the in-box. This means that once you genuinely resolve the cloud hanging around a traumatic event from years ago, that cloud is over, done, released.

And this is true whether or not we are aware of it. Stefanie was not consciously aware that her parents' scolding over that quarter was still sitting in her in-box fifty years later, but there it sat, waiting for closure. Once she went through the Four-Step Process, it was *gone*.

Your Empowering Belief

Earlier we said that we literally grow our beliefs out of new nerve pathways, like a dynamic topiary of the mind. Here is the even more radical corollary: if we can grow them, then we can *regrow* them. That is, we can intentionally grow *new* beliefs.

Step 3 is where you erase negative life beliefs and install positive new ones.

To prepare for this, first we'll have you bring up the self-limiting belief you identified in step 1 and transform it into an opposite, self-empowering belief. For example, if your strongest self-limiting belief is "I am not safe," then the opposite, self-empowering belief might be "I am completely safe and secure."

Here is a list of the seven common self-limiting beliefs together with their positive corollaries.

I am not safe.	→	I am completely safe and secure, and everything is okay.
I am worthless.	→	I am worthy and deserving of all success.
I am powerless.	→	I am powerful and capable.

I am not lovable.	→	I am a loving person and am loved.
I cannot trust anyone.	→	I am surrounded by trusting and trustworthy friends.
I am bad.	→	I bring value to everyone I meet.
I am alone.	→	I am a child of God/of the universe.

You might reword these, depending on your situation. Whether you come up with your own version or simply use one of the statements above, now we want you to write down your new empowering belief so that you'll have ready access to it. You'll be using it shortly.

Statement of Self-Acceptance

The next element in this step is a simple statement of self-acceptance:

I fully and deeply accept myself.

There are a number of reasons this simple statement is so powerful and fundamental. Self-acceptance is a *superordinate* concept, that is, it is in a class by itself. It trumps any other affirmation you might make. Whether it is confidence, self-esteem, strength of resolve, sureness of ability, or any other capacity, whatever it is you would like to affirm and build into your life, it has to start from a platform of self-acceptance.

Part of the reason this is so is that, before you can set a course for a new destination, you have to know your starting point. Accepting yourself as you are puts you in the here and now. Until you have that clear starting point, any journey is going to be handicapped. If you don't accept something, it's extremely difficult to change it, because you can't fight something and change it at the same time.

The vast majority of people who are in distress, wanting to change their lives, do *not* accept themselves because they fear that doing so would mean affirming those same negative qualities or circumstances they wish to change. But that isn't how it works. Denial leaves you powerless. Acceptance empowers you.

Accepting yourself does not mean being satisfied with the status quo or giving up any hope of improvement. Quite the opposite: deep and full self-acceptance puts you in the driver's seat, in a position of strength. It puts you in a place from which it becomes possible to change and grow powerfully.

Often we tend to identify with our circumstances, and especially with our most challenging circumstances. If we have an illness, a damaged relationship, a financial hardship, we may start to feel that problem *is* us. But deep self-acceptance means I am *not* the disease, I am *not* the divorce, I am *not* the financial setback. Whatever is going on in my life is not who I am, it is simply what I am passing through at the moment.

Another way of saying this is that this statement moves you from an *external locus of control* to an *internal locus of control*. Starting from a place of self-acceptance is a reclamation of your self-efficacy.

I fully and deeply accept myself.

There are many meanings and interpretations you can give to this statement. Here are just a handful of the infinite number of ways one might express deep self-acceptance:

I deeply accept things the way they are, as a place to start.

I fully accept myself, even with whatever faults or shortcomings I have and knowing that there are things I want to change.

I completely embrace myself, all that I have been and all that I will be, with all my imperfections and all my limitless potential.

I fully accept myself as a child of God.

I fully accept myself as a spiritual being.

I fully accept myself as a being in the universe.

All of these are right and all of them are fine, and if you want to create another version of this idea just for yourself, feel free to do so. For our step 3, we like to use the simplest, clearest, most comprehensive statement we can. It's also important that whatever your statement of self-acceptance is, it's very easy to remember, so that you don't have to refer to something written when you are going through the step.

I fully and deeply accept myself.

"What if this statement just doesn't ring true for me?" clients sometimes ask us. What if you really don't feel that you *can* accept yourself?

That's okay; we're going to have you go ahead and say it anyway. If you are in a place right now where you feel you cannot accept yourself, just consider that as part of the circumstance you're including in your statement of self-acceptance.

Your Personal Code to Joy

Now we'll add these two elements together to create what we call your *personal code to joy*. Starting with this statement of self-acceptance, we simply add to it a statement of your own self-empowering belief. For example:

I deeply and fully accept myself, and I feel safe and secure in my life.

I deeply and fully accept myself, and I feel loved and deserving of love.

I deeply and fully accept myself. I am competent, capable, and worthy.

This combination of words—a simple statement of self-acceptance together with your new self-empowering belief—is powerful.

Now think about what this relates to in your life. When you say "safe," for example, are you mainly thinking about your physical safety in the neighborhood where you live, or where you work? Your physical health? Your relationships? Feeling safe in social situations? Whatever the context is for you, hold those issues in mind as you make the statement.

If you like, you can also personalize the statement itself, making it more specific to your situation.

I deeply and fully accept myself, and I am capable in my work as a [whatever your profession is].

I deeply and fully accept myself, and I am fully at ease in social situations.

I deeply and fully accept myself, and I completely deserve a long, loving, and happy marriage.

Again, though, for your present purposes it is best if this statement is short, simple, and easy to remember. For now, as you are first learning the Four-Step Process, we recommend that you use one of these seven versions:

Examples of a Personal Code to Joy

I deeply and fully accept myself. I am safe and everything is okay.

I deeply and fully accept myself. I am worthy and deserving of all success.

I deeply and fully accept myself. I am powerful and capable.

I deeply and fully accept myself. I am loving and I am loved.

I deeply and fully accept myself. I am surrounded by trusting, trustworthy friends.

I deeply and fully accept myself. I bring value to everyone I meet.

I deeply and fully accept myself. I am a child of God/of the universe.

Pledge of Acceptance

As powerful as this statement is, it is still only a statement on the cognitive level. In other words, this is your flea speaking. Now we need to bring your elephant into alignment. Where the real power comes into play is by opening a channel to your subconscious, which we access through your biofield.

This is the purpose of the next element of this step, which we call the *pledge:*

- Place your right hand over your heart, as if you were saying the American Pledge of Allegiance.

There is a nerve bundle located here, in the intercostal space between the second and third ribs, lying just beneath your fingertips. If you press or rub this spot, it will typically feel a little tender. We call this the *repatterning spot:* rubbing this spot triggers a neurolymphatic response that functions something like a major acupoint.

Don't worry if you are not sure whether you've located the exact right spot. Firm pressure in this general area above your heart will activate the nerve bundle and produce the desired effect.

- Rub this *repatterning spot* in a clockwise motion with the flats of the fingertips of your right hand.
- As you rub this area, repeat *your personal code to joy,* either aloud or silently to yourself, five times.

Rubbing this nerve bundle opens a gateway to the biofield, allowing your statement to enter you and sink in on a far deeper level.

You might think of it this way: imagine you are using an ATM to get some cash from your checking account. You have just put in your card, so the machine knows who you are—but that's not enough to complete the transaction and get out the cash. What's missing? You still have to key in your password, key in the amount you want, and press ENTER.

In our exercise, your statement of self-acceptance is the password; your self-empowering belief is like telling the machine how much cash you want the machine to give you; and rubbing the *repatterning spot* is equivalent to pressing the ENTER key.

> *Password = "I deeply and fully accept myself . . ."*
>
> *Withdrawal request = "and I am completely safe and secure."*
>
> *Pressing ENTER = rubbing repatterning spot*

This *pledge of acceptance* and *personal code to joy* form the center of step 3. It is the meat of the sandwich, wrapped between slices of imagery that speak to your subconscious. The first image, which came before the *pledge of acceptance*, was the *healing basket*. Now it's time to create the images that come after the pledge and wrap this step all together.

Images of Your Ideal Life

The final element in step 3 is to bring to your mind images of your life as you would like it to be—to visualize what you want to have working in your life.

The goal here is to have you see the life you described in your self-empowering belief. This could mean imagining scenes from your ideal life, as if it you were watching a movie about you. Or, it could mean imagining individual images, like snapshots or movie stills. And this does not necessarily have to be purely visual, or even to be visual at all. You can bring up sensations, feelings, sounds, smells, whatever sense impressions vividly evoke the life you genuinely want to be living:

> *The smell of something baking*
>
> *The feel of someone's skin*
>
> *The chill of new-fallen snow on the ski slopes*
>
> *The cool, salty spray of surf in your honeymoon or vacation*

The point is to evoke a sense or feeling that connects to the positive emotion you experience in your new life, the life you are letting loose by unblocking and letting go of old limitations.

As you brainstorm, if you feel it is helpful, you can jot down a list of words or phrases that will bring back to mind the images that are coming to you. Remember, though, it's not the words you're looking for: it is the *feelings*.

There is a good chance that the roots of your self-limiting beliefs lay in experiences that happened so early in life that you had not yet developed the language of words to describe them. If those beliefs have been embedded in your being as preverbal emotions, then it stands to reason that the most powerful way to replace them is with new, positive, empowering emotions—feelings that go beyond words.

There is an expression in the world of sales: "People buy on emotion, then rationalize it after the fact with logic"—and this is especially true of your subconscious mind. It will "buy" the idea of your empowered, positive, powerful, joyful, fulfilling life far more readily through the language of image and emotion than it will through any logical or rational argument.

You can speak the words, "I am having a loving and fulfilling relationship," until the cows come home. But give your subconscious mind the salt scent of the surf, the feel of the wet sand between your toes, the sound of your lover's laughter and the sensation of his or her fingers intertwined with yours as you walk the beach together—that collection of images far outweighs any verbal affirmation you could possibly come up with!

This is similar to the process often taught as creative visualization, positive thinking, or affirmation—but with a crucial difference.

As we said earlier, if you don't first clear the resistance in your biofield and subconscious, then when you practice positive thinking, affirmations, or creative visualization, what can easily happen is that you simply end up arguing with yourself. Even as you consciously repeat,

"Every day, in every way, I am getting better and better . . . ," your sub-conscious mind is muttering, "Oh, really? I don't *think* so!"—and in contests of will between conscious and subconscious, you already know which one wins.

The crucial difference here is that before even getting to this part of the process, you have taken the necessary steps to reorganize your body's energy so that it is in alignment with your intention rather than fighting it, and you have "emptied the cup" of emotional and energetic charge surrounding the negative past experiences and self-limiting belief you identified earlier.

You have prepared the soil for these seeds of positivity to take root, sprout, and flourish.

Variations

Imagery can be a very personal thing. Over the years we have had clients who have customized the basic elements of step 3 in all sorts of ways. Again, when you are first learning the sequence and elements of the four steps, we strongly recommend that you keep it as simple as possible. Even if you never vary it and use only the very basic default images and language we are providing here, it will still be intensely personal because of the experiences, memories, feelings, and ideal life images you bring to it.

However, we thought it would also be helpful to share with you some of the most common variants and additions to the process that we have worked with over the years. Consider all these as options: some of them may especially appeal to you or strike you as helpful to you, and others may not.

Variant: Images of Release

In addition to letting the healing basket gradually disappear, it can be helpful to bring up specific images of cleansing or letting go, such as:

- Standing under a waterfall and letting it wash away all your nega-tive beliefs and past hurts and cares

- Walking or dancing in the rain and letting it cleanse and purify you
- Dunking in a pure mountain lake
- Swimming underwater and having all negative beliefs washed away
- Standing in a warm shower and watching the old beliefs swirl down the drain
- Standing in a beam of cleansing, healing light shining down from the heavens

Another way to do this is to write down on a piece of paper the negative elements you want to release, and place the paper into a bowl or other container, then bury the container or throw it away. Or, put the paper in a fireplace or candle and let it burn. You might write a few key words with a felt-tip pen on a helium-filled balloon, then release it outside and watch it float away. Adding some physical action to the imagery can be a powerful way to blend the mind and body experience of letting go.

These are rituals of release: by defining, containing, and then letting go of these negative elements, you give your subconscious permission to release them.

Variant: Making the Healing Journey

Imagine traveling from a starting point A (where you've been) to a given destination, point B (your ideal life), in whatever way gives you the greatest sense of peace and contentment. It doesn't matter what form or context you choose; whatever feels most natural and right to you is best.

Some like to envision themselves making their healing journey as a run or a jog. Some like to walk along a beach, or hike a trail through the woods. Some envision golfing and carrying their bag of clubs with them; others ski. It's completely up to you.

As you work your way from point A to point B, let yourself pass through a beautiful environment that you enjoy. As you go, imagine the trees, rocks, shrubs, whatever scenery naturally occurs there.

This is not idle aesthetics or just a "relaxation" technique. Remember, images are the language of the subconscious. This is a powerful tool to aid in the dissolving and disappearing of a lingering fog of distress that may have held you in its clutches for decades.

This scenery can become a cue to evoke the Zeigarnik effect and "close any open files," that is, to resolve any unresolved issues. These trees, hills, and any other scenery you pass on your healing journey represent the feelings and circumstances that are part of the issues you are letting go of. This is not something you need to dwell on. You don't need to dig down into those feelings or issues or stop to examine them. Just notice the scenery in passing and keep walking, jogging, or skiing. The simple act of noticing them is what effectively closes those files and deletes those issues from your psyche's in-box.

Variant: Locate the Feeling

You can assist the process by locating the specific energy center within your biofield where the issues you're releasing most resonate.

This is easier to do than it might sound. It's much like placing your hand on your head and slowly moving it about to discern the location of a headache.

As you think about the negative beliefs, feelings, or past experiences you want to let go of, place your hand on different locations of your body to see where that residue seems to resonate most. You might feel it just below the beltline, in your belly, in your solar plexus, your chest, your throat, or your head.

There are some common qualities that often resonate in particular areas. For example, issues of safety, security, and confidence often resonate deep in the belly; anger or jealousy in the solar plexus; lovesickness, heartbreak, loneliness, and grief in the heart; and issues around self-expression, being heard or listened to, in the throat area.

Common Issues and Corresponding Energy Centers

Throat	→	Expression, identity
Heart	→	Love, heartbreak, loneliness, relationship issues
Solar plexus	→	Anger, jealousy, envy, resentment
Belly	→	Safety, confidence, strength, presence

Close your eyes, and imagine sending healing energy to the area where you feel that distress or blockage. For some, this can be a powerful reinforcement. Again, though, this is an optional addition to the process, not an essential element.

Variant: Address Your Executive Function

You can identify your own internal executive function by giving it a name so that you can address it directly. We have had clients who decided to call their inner executive "Boss," "Soul," "Friend," "Inner Healer," or even a personal name like "Sam" or "Susan."

Once you've chosen the name you're going to use, address your executive function directly and ask it to help clear out whatever is in your healing basket. If you decide to call it Soul, for example, then you might say:

"Soul, please gather up and release any old material from the past that's in the way of my ideal life."

The key here is that your being already knows how to heal itself. When you inadvertently get a cut or a scrape, your body knows how to heal it. Your immune system knows how to deal with an infection. You don't need to consciously give your body all the specific instructions about *how* to heal: *it knows*.

The psyche also knows how to self-heal naturally, if you give it the right nutrients and alignment. You don't have to give it all the detailed instructions. Once you establish the intention to heal, you can trust that your mind and body know how to do the healing. All you need to do consciously is focus your intention on the positive outcome.

Addressing your executive function is a way of stepping into your own shoes to set your healing journey in motion. Imagine the change of belief and perception that you want to effect in yourself, and then ask your healing mind to go into your subconscious and create that repatterning. It knows what to do: just ask.

Variant: Images of Adulthood

You can use a common, everyday tool of adulthood as a powerful image to evoke the fact that you are now an adult and are fully capable of interpreting events objectively. In other words, while things that happened in your childhood may have cast a cloud over your life, if those same events happened today, as an adult you would deal with them very differently—and by evoking images of adulthood you can reclaim executive function and reinterpret those past events.

An authority figure, bully, or other figure in your life who held power over you when you were four or seven has *no* power over you today, and these images of adulthood help to trigger your psyche to remember that.

For example, close your eyes and imagine holding your car keys in one hand and a credit card in the other. If your profession involves a clearly identified tool—for a race car driver or pilot, a steering wheel or plane controls; for a surgeon, a scalpel—then you might use that as well, as long as does not have complicating childhood associations.

Our favorite image of adulthood is car keys, in part because you hold them in your hand so often that the feeling is usually easy to imagine vividly.

For example, as you are putting past events and old feelings into your healing basket, you can imagine the feel of your car keys in your hand:

this tells you that you are an adult now, and those old feelings have no power over you any longer.

This image can serve as a kind of anchor throughout your day, as well, so that every time you pick up your car keys, your entire being is reminded that you are living a new life now:

you are safe;

you are worthy;

you are powerful and capable;

you are loving and are loved;

you are surrounded by trusting, trustworthy friends;

you bring value to everyone you meet;

and you are not alone—you are a child of God, a child of the universe.

Step 3: Repattern

Purpose: Release negative beliefs and install new empowering beliefs in their place.

a. Healing basket (three minutes)

- Visualize a *healing basket* or other container of your choosing.

- Place into it all the negative elements from step 1.

- Over the next three minutes or so, visualize it gradually disappearing or floating away, taking all those negative elements with it.

b. Pledge of acceptance (about one minute)

- Place your right hand over your heart and with the tips of your fingers locate the *repatterning spot* (between second and third ribs).

- While rubbing this spot in a clockwise motion, repeat your *personal code to joy*—a statement of self-acceptance plus your self-empowering belief—aloud or silently, five times.

c. Images from your ideal life (several minutes)

- For the next few minutes, visualize scenes and impressions from your empowered, joyful life.

d. Options

- Images of release

- Images of healing journey

- Locate the feeling (energy centers)

- Name and directly address your executive function

- Images of adulthood

CHAPTER SIX

Anchoring

Just click your heels together three times
and say, "There's no place like home."
—Glinda, in *The Wizard of Oz*

AS SIMPLE AS THEY may appear, the steps you've taken up to this point in the process are *powerful*, and their impact goes deep. Remember Chantal in Rwanda, Keith, the Vietnam vet, and the thousands of other subjects in the various studies we looked at in chapter 4? Once their nightmares, flashbacks, and other symptoms were gone, they were *gone*: even months and years later, they had not returned.

When you identify an issue and root out its source, pinpoint the underlying negative belief, clear your system and reorganize your electrical polarity, contain and dissolve those negative elements, and replace them with new positive beliefs reinforced by vivid images of your new fulfilling, empowered life, then you have not just lightly touched on that issue—you have profoundly changed it.

But we're not quite finished yet: there's one more step.

Steps 1 through 3 create some deep changes in the way you see yourself and your world. The purpose of step 4 is to establish and drive your new self-empowering beliefs and thought patterns firmly into your being, so that they become an embedded, permanent part of who you are.

Step 4 introduces two new elements to the process: a simple exercise we call the *anchoring hold*, and your personal *symbol of balance*. Let's look at both of these in turn.

The Anchoring Hold

To perform the anchoring hold, simply place one hand on your forehead, as if you were feeling for a fever, and the other hand in the opposite position, cupping the back of your head.

Anchoring Hold

Well known in such disciplines as craniosacral therapy and chiropractic as the *frontal-occipital hold* (or simply *F/O hold*), this deceptively simple position works powerfully on a number of levels at once.

First, we are mildly increasing blood flow to the prefrontal cortex (front area of the brain), stimulating the areas responsible for imagination and our capacity to envision our future. At the same time, we are also stimulating circulation to the occipital or rear portion of the brain, where the vision center is located. Increasing blood flow increases function.

Holding the forehead is a natural destressing gesture that we all know intuitively. If you've ever taken care of a child who was ill, you've probably had this experience: you automatically place your hand on the child's forehead. Yes, it's one way to check for a fever—but more than that, it's also soothing and calming. We instinctively do the same thing to ourselves, too. For example, if we receive some shocking news, we might place our hand on our own forehead as we exclaim, "Holy cow!" (or whatever other expletive pops out), and sink into our chair.

In addition to blood circulation, we're directly addressing key functions in our biofield. For one thing, the areas of the face and back of the head are both rich in acupoints, lying along several different key meridians, that have a calming and centering effect.

In a more general way, we are also treating the energy center corresponding to our head and brain. In previous chapters we talked about the various energy centers of the body (traditionally called *chakras*, from the Sanskrit word for "wheel"). The anchoring hold is a way of literally holding one of these centers in the palms of your hands. Each chakra or energy center has a distinct character and is associated with a different set of functions and effects on our overall well-being, as we explored briefly in chapter 5. There, however, we looked at the four centers of the belly, solar plexus, heart, and throat. Here we are dealing with the energy center of the brain itself.

The effects of charging and balancing this specific center include:

- Putting the past in perspective
- Getting grounded in the now
- Gaining a clearer picture of one's future

The anchoring hold, in other words, helps to anchor the shift in thinking, beliefs, and mental images that we are working to effect through the Four-Step Process itself.

In terms of imagery—and remember, images are the language of the subconscious—we are also evoking a strong sense of *containment*, much as we did with the healing basket image in step 3, except that in this case, we are containing our new self-empowering beliefs and the scenes of our ideal life that we played out at the end of step 3. Just before step 4, we have evoked powerful pictures of the life we want to be living; now we are, in a literal sense, *holding that thought.*

Thus the anchoring hold works powerfully on the energetic level, the cognitive level, the metaphoric and subconscious level, and the physiological level, all at the same time.

Your Personal Symbol of Balance

Your personal *symbol of balance* is a single image that, for you, represents your triumph over past limitations or challenges. It is a symbol of the new abilities, deepened capacities, or other values and qualities that lie at the core of those scenes from your ideal life. It represents all that you stand to gain by clearing away past blocks and limitations, embracing your own self-efficacy, and creating your fulfilling life as you wish it to be.

We use the word *balance* to refer to this image because whatever specific values, strengths, or other qualities you want to create in your new life—self-confidence, love, financial success, a sense of security and safety, patience and a sense of being relaxed, or whatever else it may be—at its heart it represents for you a "new normal," a new and more fulfilling, satisfying picture of everyday life. In other words, it is a new level of homeostasis, a new state of balance.

We will have more to say about the virtues of balance in chapter 8, but for now, we'll just say that balance is the essential value that underlies all the aims of the Four-Step Process. Electrically speaking, for example, we are bringing into balance your left and right hemispheres, left and right sides of the body, and all negative and positive polarities within your biofield. We are bringing into alignment the goals and focus of both your conscious attention and your subconscious faculties. We are also bringing into balance mental and physical, external and internal, as well as past and future.

There are three common images that we like to offer as default symbols for this step, each representing balance in a different domain of life:

1. The *heart*, representing balance in love, relationships, and all interpersonal exchange
2. The *dollar sign*, representing financial balance and success, as well as a harmonious, successful state of balance in relation to work, career, and your personal resources in general
3. The *rod of Asclepius*, the traditional symbol of health, to refer to physiological health and personal strength and balance

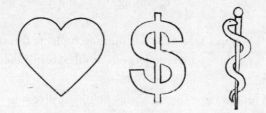

Here are some further examples of symbols our clients have adopted over the years as their personal symbols of balance:

The horizon

Sunset over the ocean

A flower

Infinity sign

Scales of justice

An acrobat on tightrope

A flamingo standing on one foot

A lion (standing for strength and courage)

A bird in flight (grace, freedom, spirit)

A lake at sunrise (peace, harmony, new beginnings)

A tree silhouetted on a hill (strength, endurance, wisdom)

A flower (love, beauty, calm)

Step 4

Now let's put these elements together. Remember, coming from step 3, you have just spent several minutes visualizing *images and scenes from your ideal life*. Step 3 merges seamlessly into step 4:

Now, as these scenes and images continue to run in your imagination, apply the *anchoring hold*, breathing slowly and deeply, for another minute.

Next, let the images fade out and continue applying the anchoring hold for another minute while you let your mind go blank and focus on your breathing.

Finally, as you continue the anchoring hold, visualize your *symbol of balance* and hold that in your mind for a minute.

Here is this step in outline form:

- Continue *images and scenes from your ideal life* and apply *anchoring hold* (one minute).
- Continue *anchoring hold* alone, mind blank, focus on breathing (one minute).
- Continue *anchoring hold* and visualize *symbol of balance* (one minute).

Coming at the end of the process, this last step takes just three minutes, yet it creates a powerful conclusion to everything that has come before and helps to set it firmly in your being.

The Next Thirty Days

However, we're *still* not quite finished. There is still one more step, *beyond* the fourth step—and that is a simple routine for integrating everything you've gained from the entire process into your life over the next thirty days and beyond.

To ensure that the changes you've made are permanent, now we're going to have you take just a few minutes out of each day, for the next thirty days (and longer, if you wish), to give yourself a condensed version of the entire process. You can think of this as a self-contained, standalone refresher course. We call it the *daily refresher.*

The Daily Refresher

- Crosshand breathing (two minutes)
- Pledge and personal code to joy statement, aloud or silent (five times)
- Anchoring hold, visualizing your symbol of balance (one minute)

For the next thirty days, do this three times a day: for example, first thing in the morning, last thing at night, and one more time in the middle of the day, such as on your lunch break.

Our purpose in step 4 is to put in place an image that sums up everything that has taken place as a result of steps 1, 2, and 3 and to seal it into your mind. But we're doing something else, too. We are also setting up a series of cues, so that over the days to come, with this very simple mini-process that takes no more than a few minutes, you can quickly evoke and *reinstall* everything you did as you worked through the entire process.

You might think of it this way:

In step 4, you are setting an anchor in the ocean floor, so that your new beliefs and thought patterns won't drift away with the currents of everyday circumstance. At the same time, life being what it is, you know that sooner or later you *are* going to drift. Inevitably, we become distracted by the events of our lives. The stronger the currents of what is going on around us, the faster and farther we are likely to drift.

So, in addition to putting down an anchor, we also use step 4 to set up a buoy on the surface of your mind that will serve as a marker, so that whenever you want to return to where that anchor is set, you can find its location immediately.

That buoy is your personal symbol of balance.

Thirty days is the minimum length of time we typically recommend for doing this, because it normally takes about thirty days for the subconscious mind to accept and incorporate a new habit.

If you are dealing with a strong trauma or painful event, such as deep grieving or a major life change, or if for any other reason you feel you need more support and reinforcement, then by all means continue this daily practice for six weeks or even longer. It can only help.

And Whenever You Feel Stressed . . .

In addition to this thirty-day daily refresher, the process gives you tools you can use anytime, anywhere, for the rest of your life, as you feel the need.

Anytime you are feeling stressed or under the gun, or feel your new positive beliefs are being challenged, there are three different miniprocesses you can use to put yourself back on track.

"But when I'm most stressed," people sometimes say, "I don't have time or the space to get by myself and do any kind of lengthy process. I can't even think straight in times like that, let alone remember some elaborate sequence!"

We know. We've experienced this, too. Things can get hectic and feel out of control sometimes. That's okay: you can still use these tools, even at times like this. We have designed these mini-processes to be extremely simple, practical tools that you can implement at any time, in any circumstance, right in the midst of your busy life.

1. Daily refresher

If you are able to take a few minutes by yourself, you can repeat the daily refresher that you did for thirty days, above. Combining elements from steps 2, 3, and 4 all together, it is a powerful set of cues that will reorganize your electrical polarity and bring back to mind all the gains of the Four-Step Process.

2. Mini-refresher

As an abbreviated version of the daily refresher, you can simply visualize your symbol of balance while applying the anchoring hold to your head.

The beauty of this symbol is that it is a single visual element—and yet, because you have used it as the conclusion to the Four-Step Process itself, it contains within it the seeds and fruits of the entire process. The subconscious mind is a powerful thing, and once you've gone through all the steps of the process, all it takes is this one carefully chosen trigger, and your subconscious can rerun the entire process without your having to follow any of it consciously.

The more often you do this, the more potent this trigger becomes. In many circumstances, applying the anchoring hold and evoking a picture of your symbol of balance for just thirty seconds is enough to reinvoke all the gains you've achieved through the full Four-Step Process.

3. Crosshand breathing

Anytime you feel off-kilter, stressed, or distressed, simply doing two minutes of crosshand breathing will calm your system and correct a reversed or disorganized polarity.

Not only is this extremely simple, it has the added practical advantage of looking innocuous to outside observers. Sometimes it just isn't practical to do the anchoring hold or pledge of acceptance, because they may prompt the people around you to ask what you're doing, or if you're okay, and so forth. But crosshand breathing is something you can practice virtually anywhere, anytime, without drawing unwanted attention.

Two minutes is ideal, but sometimes you don't have two minutes. That's okay, too. Often just one minute will be sufficient to effect a positive change.

Anchoring and Addictions

One of the most intriguing and promising areas where we have used the Four-Step Process is with people who have deeply ingrained patterns of

addictive and compulsive behaviors—and this is an area that clearly il-
lustrates the value and the power of the daily refresher.

Over the years, clients have come to us with hundreds of such issues,
including compulsive eating or dieting, habitual binging and purging,
alcohol and drug addiction, compulsive spending and shopping, gam-
bling problems, sexual addiction, obsessive thinking, pornography and
Internet addiction, and many others.

Again, we want to repeat here the disclaimer at the front of this book:
We are not offering this process as a way to treat major clinical problems, such as severe chemical addictions or major depressive or anxiety
disorders. *Code to Joy* is aimed at issues of everyday life that so many
suffer with. For severe addictions and those that have a strong chemical and physiological basis (such as addictions to alcohol, narcotics, and
hard drugs), a multi-team approach is typically needed to completely
resolve the problem, which may include such elements as hospitalization
and detoxification, a twelve-step support group, medical treatment programs, or other strategies.

However, even in these more difficult cases, the underlying emotional dynamic that first set the addictive process in motion is something the Four-Step Process *can* help address, often saving the person
years of relapsing to old behaviors.

People suffering with these more severe clinical issues typically have
the same negative, self-limiting beliefs lying at the core of the issues
they're dealing with—beliefs about their safety, self-worth, lovability,
powerlessness, isolation, and so forth—as does everyone else. Addressing these issues with the Four-Step Process is in some ways much like
addressing any other patterns of distress in one's life. The Four-Step
Process is especially useful because it quickly allows the person to have
greater emotional clarity about why he or she has the addiction. Once
a person realizes the cause, it becomes easier to come to grips with the
situation, come to a clear decision, and make a strong commitment to
make a lasting change.

In these situations, when there is such a strong pull to lapse into the old patterns, it is especially important to incorporate some elements of the process into a daily routine. In our experience, the person overcoming an addictive pattern will want to repeat the daily refresher three times a day at least, and continue to do so as a daily routine for a good two or three months even *after* the core issue is resolved, in order to fully root out the old patterns and anchor the new beliefs more firmly.

Jason's Habit

Jason was in his last year in college when he started growing anxious about the career path decisions he would soon be making. As graduation approached, his anxiety grew to the point where he could not unwind enough to get to sleep at night. Some friends gave him some pot to relax him.

Jason had used marijuana intermittently before, but now it became a crutch he relied on every night. Within a few weeks, the habitual pot use made him depressed and despondent. Rather than getting clearer on his career path, he started feeling even *less* capable of making these big decisions. This in turn fueled his anxieties further—leading to ever-greater pot use. He knew he was in a vicious cycle and digging himself in deeper every night, but he felt powerless to do anything about it.

When he began working with the Four-Step Process, Jason was quickly able to identify the negative *I am powerless* belief underlying his downward-spiraling mood, together with several events early in his life that had first sparked that belief. Within minutes, his sense of anxiety about his career choices, together with the feeling of hopeless despondency that had taken root, dissolved its grip, and Jason felt dramatically like his old self.

However, Jason admitted, he honestly didn't know if he could let go of his new crutch. He *wanted* to quit smoking pot, and the underlying reason that had drawn him to it in the first place had dissipated, but still, the habit felt like it was stuck to him—"like Super Glue," as he put it.

We suggested that he take a few minutes to go through the daily refresher four times every day—on arising, before sleeping, and two more times during the day—and that in addition, he practice two minutes of crosshand breathing anytime he felt things getting out of control.

Jason followed this routine faithfully, and within the first few days he began feeling a significant shift in his sense of confidence. However, he continued smoking pot every night. Nevertheless, he stuck doggedly to his routine of four daily refreshers every day.

After another week, he was able to get to sleep one night *without* smoking pot, and a few days later he did so again, and then several days in a row. By the end of week 4, he had completely stopped using pot and he felt like a new person—which, in a sense, he was.

A Smoker's Story

Margey had smoked at least a pack and a half of cigarettes daily for the past twenty-five years. A few years before we saw her, she had managed to stop for a few weeks, but when the stress levels at her workplace began increasing, she had started again and had not been able to quit or even cut back since.

Margey was becoming short of breath and was deeply worried about her health.

"I'm in my fifties," she told us, "and I know I have to start taking better care of myself. I'm ready to do this." She didn't really think it would work, but she was determined to give it a serious try anyway.

Aside from the health concerns, Margey also hated the fact that she seemed so utterly incapable of making this change that she knew she needed to make. The feeling of powerlessness was very frustrating for her.

When Margey first went through the Four-Step Process, it immediately shifted her emotional state. She soon began seeing this as a real possibility.

As with any addictions that have a chemical basis, we advised her to repeat the daily refresher at least three or four times a day—and she did. She used no nicotine gum, no patch, no other external support.

How long it takes to get relief from an addiction like cigarettes varies greatly from person to person. In Margey's case, it took three weeks.

Within a week of our visit, she had dropped from a pack and a half a day to a handful of cigarettes a day. After another week, she got down to one or two a day, and by the end of the following week, to nothing. She was ecstatic.

Her husband, who still smoked himself, was astonished. And this is where the story becomes especially poignant.

You'll recall Steve Hopkins, the successful sales director who suffered every time he had to sit through a social event. Through the Four-Step Process, Steve not only was able to relax and enjoy his evenings with friends, family, and colleagues, he also realized he could now fly on commercial airlines instead of feeling forced to spend a fortune leasing private jets every time he had to travel.

One detail we did not mention about Steve's story was how he first came to see us: we had helped his wife Margey quit smoking.

And that is not the end of Steve's story. The day he called to tell us how well he was doing, he started thinking about what else he might change in his life. That night, he wrote an entry in his journal, which he shared with us some months later:

Next up, consider quitting the little cigars. Not sure I am ready for this yet, but want to consider it. Would allow my running and tennis stamina to improve, and make it easier to find a hotel room. And make me more steady/peaceful during the day.

At the time, Steve was smoking cigarillos (his "little cigars") throughout the day. We asked him a question: If he *did* stop smoking, what would he be able to do that he wasn't already doing?

"That's easy," he replied immediately. "Long-distance running. I used to do it, and I love it—but I can't go back to it as long as I'm smoking these cigarillos. That would be a wonderful gift to give myself."

Then we asked him how he would like to start the process, knowing that it would go better if he was the one calling the shots, and not us.

However, we misunderstood a key piece of his answer. We *thought* he said that he was accustomed to having a cigarillo in the middle of the day, and that he wanted to start the quitting process by eliminating that midday smoke. We took him through the Four-Step Process again, focusing on issues surrounding his perceived powerlessness to stop smoking, and (as we had with Margey) suggested that he practice the daily refresher several times daily in the days to come.

We talked with him a week later, and asked him how it was going.

"Well," he said, "we've been totally successful."

How so? we asked. Had he completely stopped smoking that midday cigar?

"Not *cigar*," he said. "*Cigars*."

Wait—*what*? We thought we were talking about quitting a *single* daily cigar as a way to get Steve's toe in the water.

"Nope," he replied. "I wasn't talking about quitting *one* of them. I was talking about quitting *all* of 'em."

Today Margey walks a good four to six miles every day, feels great about herself and her life, and doesn't smoke—and neither does Steve.

Step 4: Anchor

Purpose: Ensure that the results of the first three steps are deep and long-lasting.

a. Anchoring hold
- Continue *scenes from your ideal life* (from step 3) and apply *anchoring hold* (one minute)
- Continue anchoring hold alone, mind blank, focused on breathing (one minute)

b. Symbol of balance
- Continue anchoring hold and visualize personal *symbol of balance* (one minute)

Additional Daily Tools
Daily Refresher
Several times daily, for the next thirty days (or as long as you like)

a. Crosshand breathing (two minutes)
b. Pledge and personal code to joy statement, aloud or silent (five times)
c. Anchoring hold, visualizing your personal symbol of balance (one minute)

Mini-Refresher
Anytime you feel stressed and need to reconnect
- Anchoring hold, visualizing your personal symbol of balance (one minute)

Crosshand Breathing
Anytime you feel distressed or that your polarity is out of balance, simply practice two or three minutes of crosshand breathing.

CHAPTER SEVEN

Taking It to the Next Level

*The further up and the further in you go, the bigger
everything gets. The inside is larger than the outside.*
—Tumnus the Faun, in *The Last Battle*, C. S. Lewis

IN MOST OF THE stories we've related in this book, we have described a single issue that the person was dealing with. Stefanie got scolded for accepting a quarter. Caitlyn's parents criticized her. Richard was called on to give an oral report in third grade. Heather's grandfather died.

In reality, things are rarely so simple. We are not one-dimensional beings, but many-layered and complex. Often we'll find there is more than a single negative belief holding sway, and likewise, there are often multiple issues going in our lives that we would like to change—even if there is just one that has our attention for the moment, and the others occur to us only later.

We see this happen all the time. Typically, people come to see us seeking relief around one specific *something* that is not working in their lives. It might be a particular fear or anxiety they have, like Caitlyn's panic about bridges and elevators, or a current crisis, like Heather's despondency over her breakup. It might be issues with their primary relationship, or their health, or something affecting their performance at work, like Richard's misery every time he gave a sermon. It might be that they are feeling overwhelmed with the pressures of work or of taking care of their kids.

Since there is a presenting issue they are most focused on, naturally that's the first thing we work on: we help them explore to see what might be the underlying negative belief, precipitating events or experiences early in their life, and go on to dissolve that issue and help them create new self-empowering beliefs and "ideal life" images that bring that new belief clearly into their lives.

But once that presenting issue is relieved, other issues often surface that were far less noticeable (or even invisible) before they dealt with the pressing issue that brought them to us in the first place.

Here is an analogy:

Let's say you have a splitting headache, a migraine. It hurts so much you can't concentrate on anything else—not work, not your family, not anything. You can't even eat or sleep.

So you seek help, and you get the migraine under control. Ahh, sweet relief. *But what's that?* you say, rubbing your hand on your jaw. Now that the migraine is gone, you notice you have a slight toothache. In fact, now that you think about it, you realize it's been nagging at you for a few weeks. Your head hurt so much, you just didn't pay any attention to the tooth.

All right, then, off to the dentist. You get the tooth filled. Wow, you feel so much better. But as you're driving home from the dentist, you realize that your back is aching. You think back, and remember doing some pretty strenuous yard work last weekend. You hadn't even realized it, but you must have pulled something.

Okay: headache's gone, toothache's gone . . . now let's deal with that back.

Of course the issues we are dealing with through the Four-Step Process typically are not as obvious or simple as an aching tooth, but they are pain of another sort, and often the deeper aches can become temporarily masked by more immediate hurts. Sometimes, those deeper aches have been hiding for years.

The Layers of Beth

Beth came to see us because she was having a terrible time sleeping. She kept thinking she heard noises outside at night and was terrified for her safety.

"It's crazy," she told us, "because we live in a really safe neighborhood. There hasn't been a break-in there for decades. What's more, we have a state-of-the-art security system. I *know* I'm not in any real danger—but that doesn't help. I still can't shake that feeling."

Beth's husband often traveled for his work, sometimes for days at a time, and Beth's fears had become so acute that whenever he was away, she more or less went sleepless all through the night.

As you have probably already guessed, when we asked Beth about her history, we soon found some early childhood experiences that had programmed her subconscious with the belief *I am not safe*. We took her through the Four-Step Process and showed her how to repeat the daily refresher at home. Within days she called to report that she was finally getting some sleep.

Three weeks later Beth made another appointment to see us.

When she came in to our office this second time, we asked if she was still having any trouble sleeping.

No, she assured us, her sleep was no longer an issue.

"All those fears? They're just *gone*. It's amazing," she said. She was here now for a totally different reason: she was worried that her husband Tom was cheating on her.

"I'm obsessed with the thought," she admitted. "Again, I know it's crazy. I really don't believe that Tom is doing anything like that—at least the rational part of me doesn't believe it. He's not behaving any differently, and I have absolutely no evidence or reason to be suspicious. But I just can't shake the thought."

What's more, she added, she realized that she had been having these nagging suspicions for some time. More than a year, in fact. It was only now that she was getting some sleep and was no longer exhausted, and that those gripping fears about her own safety were no longer an issue, that these jealous thoughts had finally surfaced.

We spent some time with Beth walking through the whole process a second time. Not surprisingly, we uncovered some additional painful experiences from her distant past and found there was an issue with her belief around her own lovability.

Beth was right: Tom wasn't being unfaithful at all. The problem was that on a deep level, she could not quite believe that he would remain faithful to her—because she could not accept the notion that *she herself was lovable enough* to deserve a loving, faithful husband.

Once Beth saw the early events that had fed this belief, she got the connection immediately, and since she already had the tools to dissolve this fog of distress, she was off and running.

But the story doesn't end there. Six months later, Beth came to see us one more time.

"I'm still sleeping fine," she reported, "and I feel great." She looked great, too—vibrant, relaxed, practically glowing. She went on to say that she had stopped having those obsessive thoughts about Tom, and their life together was great as well.

So, what brought her here now?

"You're going to laugh," she said, "but now that I'm feeling so much calmer and more relaxed, I've been wondering . . . well, about whether I'm really in the right job."

A successful copywriter for a small marketing firm, Beth was good at what she did, but she was starting to face the fact that deep down, the work did not feel truly fulfilling.

"I keep thinking," she added, "what should I really be *doing* with my life?"

Now that Beth had resolved the more acute issues that had been nag-

ging at her—her migraine and toothache, so to speak—she was getting down to a deeper issue. She had a feeling of powerlessness and a real question about her own worth, and it had been preventing her from doing what she truly wanted to do—which, as it turned out, was to work as an environmental journalist.

For Beth, this was in fact the most significant issue in her life. However, as long as she was too anxious about her own safety to get any sleep, or obsessed with worry that her husband was cheating on her, she didn't have the time or luxury even to think about existential questions like her life's purpose or whether she was making a positive difference in the world. Once these issues were resolved, she was able to take her life to the next level.

Unwrapping Your Gift

Sometimes, as we saw in the case of David the journalist or Steve Hopkins's long-standing neck pain, clearing one issue has the happy side effect of clearing up others as well, even without putting any specific focus on those other issues.

More often, though, people use the Four-Step Process a number of times in sequence, as Beth did, starting with the most obvious or pressing issue and then going back through the process again for another, and another.

You might go through the acute or presenting issue and find that, once it is resolved, you feel much better and don't feel the need to do any further work with the process . . . for now. Yet after a while, like Beth, you may notice or become aware of something else you want to work on. You might find yourself wanting to pick this book up again a few weeks from now, or a few months from now.

The beauty of it is that with each subsequent pass, the process becomes easier and may even feel more powerful.

For one thing, you are becoming more familiar with it each time you go through it. For another, the more dust and debris you clear away, the

more clearly you will be able to see what else needs work. With each new issue you clear, you start feeling lighter and more optimistic and have more energy and more confidence, and this naturally snowballs into finding more benefits and positive changes.

Like Beth, you may find a number of layers to unwrap—two, three, four, or even more. Take it one step at a time, and enjoy the journey! Think of this process as unwrapping a gift. There may be many layers of wrapping paper to get through, but the gift inside is worth it.

What is that gift? That gift is *you*—you and your genuine life.

Buried Treasure

The Four-Step Process is incredibly useful for alleviating problems, addressing crises, and solving even the thorniest of dilemmas. But that's only the beginning. Because your life is far more than the sum of the problems you solve: your life is a tapestry of possibilities.

You can also use the Four-Step Process to improve in any area of your life where you would like to see improvement and clear away the barriers to the full life you could be living. Wherever you are, in your relationships, in career, finances, productivity, creativity, or any other area of your life, you can clear whatever's in the way of operating at and fulfilling your fullest potential.

People often assume they are operating at pretty close to their optimum, or, at worst, at perhaps 50 percent of their potential. "I know things aren't perfect," we often hear clients say, "but on a scale of zero to ten, I figure I must be functioning at, say, at least a six."

Our experience shows something quite different. From what we've seen in the course of using neuromuscular feedback with thousands of clients, most people have an enormous amount more untapped potential than they realize.

In our practice, we often see very high-functioning people—professional athletes, accomplished businesspeople, media personalities, and so forth. And even within this unusually high-performing crowd, it is *ex-*

tremely rare to find someone operating at even 50 percent capacity. In our experience, a reasonably happy, reasonably successful person is typically operating at something like 12 percent of potential—and that's the *upper* end of the scale. For most people, 5 percent seems to be about the norm.

Just 5 percent.

Imagine the possibilities. Imagine if you were right now operating at 5 percent of what you are capable of, and you were able to increase that, not to 100 percent, not to 50 percent, but just to *20 percent*.

You'd have *quadrupled*.

Imagine being four times as clear, four times as relaxed, four times as confident. Imagine the impact this could have on your overall energy level and sense of well-being. On your immune function and ability to resist illness. On your effectiveness at work. On your relationships. On your sense of fulfillment, happiness, and joy in living.

In our experience, none of this is an unreasonable expectation. There is a vast world of fulfillment and satisfaction out there, just waiting to be enjoyed.

We call this "buried treasure," and the Four-Step Process is both map and shovel that will help you dig it up.

What Potential Are You Currently Tapping?

If you want, you can get a sense of where you currently are, in terms of the amount of your full potential that you are realizing right now in your everyday life. How? Through neuromuscular feedback.

We've using neuromuscular feedback to identify the past experiences and self-limiting beliefs that have had the most impact on you. What if we tried using the same procedure to quantify your untapped potential?

In fact, this is easy to do, and we do it all the time with our clients.

Just as you did in chapter 3, you'll need a partner to work with. First, set yourself up by going through the basic process we described in that chapter:

- *Neutralize the system.* Take both yourself and your partner through two minutes of crosshand breathing to ensure that both of your electrical polarities are properly organized.
- *Get the feel of it.* Have your partner press down on your outstretched arm, fingers over wrist, just firmly enough to feel the resistance.
- *Calibrate.* Test several sets of objective true/false statements: "My name is . . . ," "Today is . . . ," "Two plus two equals four/Two plus two equals seven," and so forth.

Once you are all set up and know your testing platform is working properly, then you're ready. Now have your partner test you while you make the following statement:

"In my [work, health, relationships, or other area of your life that you want to explore], I am operating at *50 percent or more* of my capacity."

If this statement tests strong, that means it is true: you *are* operating at 50 percent or higher. If it tests weak, then it's false: you are *not* operating at 50 percent or higher.

In that case, now step it back to 40:

"In my [same area of life] I am operating at *40 percent or more* of my capacity."

If this tests weak (that is, you are *not* operating at 40 percent potential or more), then test the same statement at 30 percent; 20 percent; 10 percent; 8 percent; and so forth. Walk it backward until you come to a number that tests strong.

Once you find a number where you test strong, then test the opposite statement as a way to confirm your results. For example, if you test strong on this statement:

"In my [whatever area of life you want to test for] I am operating at *10 percent or more* of capacity."

Then test this:

"In my [same area of life] I am *not* operating at 10 percent or more of capacity."

If the earlier statement tested strong, this statement (its opposite) should test weak.

One you have pinpointed a specific numeric level, jot that number down so you can keep track of it. As you go through the Four-Step Process, and in the days ahead as you continue to go through the daily refresher, you should see that number increase. We have seen people's actively realized potential, as measured by neuromuscular feedback, jump dramatically, sometimes even in just a period of minutes, after going through this process of clearing away the barriers to greater performance and installing new, empowering beliefs into their nervous systems.

Rob's Crisis

In the course of our practice, we have worked with hundreds of athletes, including some world champions and Olympic medalists. But one story especially touched us, because it was not only about breaking through some roadblocks in performance, but about helping a boy get his life back.

When Rob's father brought him to see us, Rob had been playing college baseball for two years. All his life, he had wanted to play baseball, and in his first year in high school he had already been pegged by his coaches as professional material. Throughout high school, Rob had worked like crazy, not only on his game but also on his academics, and his efforts had not been in vain: against considerable odds, he had managed to win admittance and a scholarship to a prestigious school that was sure to cement his future in the sport.

However, in his freshman college year, disaster struck. An ugly incident occurred on campus, and although Rob had not been involved at all, through a series of terrible events he ended up being saddled with the blame for what had happened. The kid who had been at the bottom of it all was an even more valuable ball player than Rob was, so even though the coaches suspected that Rob had been unjustly accused, they made no effort to set the record straight. There was no outright illegality involved, and Rob was not overtly punished, but the injustice of the whole sequence of events threw him into a tailspin.

Suddenly, Rob was unable to focus on his game. His grades tanked. He became depressed, angry on the field and moody elsewhere. He broke up with his girlfriend. Partway into his sophomore year, Rob was put on suspension for a series of minor but escalating disciplinary infractions. He started talking about giving up on baseball. And it wasn't just his game that was at risk. Rob was clearly on a self-destructive track.

The family thought about filing a lawsuit but worried that doing so would be tough on Rob's career too, because he might be tainted as a troublemaker. Instead, his parents helped him transfer to another school, hoping that he would be able to put the situation behind him. But the problem traveled with him to the new environment, and he still couldn't play or focus on his studies.

When Rob's parents first brought him to see us, it had been about a year since the incident and its unfortunate aftermath. In just twelve months' time, everything in his life had spiraled rapidly downward.

As we worked with Rob, we found that, sure enough, this incident resonated with an earlier incident, at the age of ten—another event where he felt he'd been unfairly accused of something he did not do. This earlier event had not been nearly as dramatic; in fact, his parents had not even been aware of it. But it had made its mark, and when this new event occurred, years later, it was such a strong resonant echo that his entire fog of distress around that earlier incident, which had been brewing for nearly a decade, came back in full force and effectively paralyzed him.

After a single session, Rob's attitude at school did an effective 180. We saw him two more times to work through some additional issues from earlier in his life and help him nail down his own follow-through practices—the daily refresher, mini-refresher, going over how to apply the whole Four-Step Process to any other issues that might come up for him in the future, and so forth—but that was it. After those three visits, he was on his own.

And he flourished. He became very successful in his new school, both academically and socially, and he got his full game back. Last time we talked with his dad, he was just breaking into the pros.

Breaking Through Ceilings

When we first saw Brad, he had gone through a series of trials: divorce, custody battle, bankruptcy, and severe tax problems. Now remarried and with a growing family, he had fought his way through all his financial problems, but was still struggling. What bothered him even more than the financial struggle itself was that he didn't understand why he kept failing to achieve his goals.

As we talked about his business and financial history, it became clear that he had repeatedly butted up against a very firm financial barrier: he was able to generate about $100,000 per year in income, but no more. Quite a few times, he'd had a great opportunity come up and been right on the cusp of something big, but either it would fall through at the last minute or he would inadvertently do something to shoot himself in the foot.

Brad is a bright and talented guy. He has good social skills and is not afraid to work hard. It would appear that he's got everything going for him.

"I ought to be experiencing all kinds of success," he told us. "Instead, it feels like everything I touch, I ruin. No matter how well I do, I always seem to wind up back at that level. It's like there is some mysterious force preventing me from getting ahead."

He was right, it was *exactly* like that—only it wasn't a mysterious force, it was the power of a negative, self-limiting belief entrenched in his subconscious mind.

This is actually quite common. We often see people who have hit an income barrier like this, when they can't seem to get past a certain earnings level, or when they do, something happens to sabotage it. If you subconsciously don't believe you are worth more than $50,000 a year, or $80,000, or $150,000, or whatever the figure is, then you will do whatever it takes to stay at that level. You may *consciously* have all kinds of motivation to do better, and all kinds of excellent reasons you would like to earn more—but wherever the elephant is headed, that's where you're going.

In that first visit, we talked about Brad's childhood and upbringing. His father had been a hard worker, had always managed to support the household and put food on the table, but just barely. "Life is tough," was the message Brad learned from his dad, who had learned it in turn from *his* father, Brad's grandfather. The core feeling in Brad's household was one of scarcity, that there was never quite enough and never would be quite enough.

As a teenager, Brad had rebelled against this generational attitude and vowed that as an adult, he was going to escape the cycle of scarcity and be highly successful.

When we used neuromuscular feedback to gauge at what level Brad was operating, we got a number of 3 percent. Incredibly, he had fought through all those difficulties, started a new family, and was managing to get by in life—at *3 percent* operating capacity! And this is not at all unusual.

We took him through the Four-Step Process, focusing on the negative belief he absorbed from his father. When he came back for a second session, he told us things had already shifted dramatically in his life.

"My wife is amazing at the change in my attitude. She asked me to tell you that it feels like she's living with a different person now—the one she originally married."

He also told us about a new opportunity that had come up during the week.

We again used neuromuscular feedback to get a sense of how far Brad had come in tapping into his own potential. This time, we got a number of 30 percent or more—*ten times* what it had been a week earlier.

This time, Brad did not blow it. That opportunity took root and blossomed into a promising new direction in his career. A year later, he was earning well over $150,000 and growing.

Of course, money is not the path to happiness. If anything, happiness is the path to money. You have to feel deserving enough, worthy enough, open enough to be able to enjoy whatever level of finances you generate and have balance in your life.

In fact, the same self-limiting dynamic that often happens around money also often happens around love and happiness. Have you ever been having a really good time with someone and heard yourself say, or felt yourself think, "This is too good to last," or some similar thought? If you stop to think about what kind belief would drive a statement like that, it would have to be something like, "I don't deserve more than a small amount of happiness . . . ,"—in other words, some version of *I'm not worthy. I'm not lovable. I don't deserve true love.*

It's those negative, self-limiting beliefs that run like bad elevator music in the background of our minds, feeding us poisonous thoughts about our own capacity and our own deservedness. They are lies, but lies that are so familiar they are nearly impossible to resist. To paraphrase the Borg from *Star Trek: The Next Generation*, "We are your subconscious: resistance is futile."

But if resistance is futile, transformation is not. We have the tools in our hands to root out, dissolve, and eliminate those rusty old negative echoes, and once we do, we can dissolve the artificial ceilings we place upon our capacity to earn income, accomplish great things, and let our lives be filled with profoundly fulfilling love relationships.

This is exactly what happened with Beth. Because she didn't believe she truly deserved the love of a wonderful, faithful husband, she had started to imagine infidelities that did not exist and was well on her way to sabotaging her marriage. Once her habitual fears and insecurities were dissolved, she and Tom went on to have the kind of joy and contentment together that they *did* truly deserve.

Tragedy into Triumph

Remember the dreams you had when you were young? Where did you imagine you would be at this point in your life, in your career, in your relationships, in your accomplishments?

So many people want to start their own businesses but shy away from following through their entire lives. So many people want to write or play music or dance or in some other way express themselves, but don't do it.

It is a quiet tragedy, all the more real for its quietness: it is the measure of buried treasure that the world never gets to see and experience. How many people don't fulfill their potential because of guilt, shame, fear, resistance, or other negative feelings generated by the rejections and hurts of their past. So many people withdraw from their own destinies and shrink from stepping into the lives they could lead, simply because of the lack of conviction that they could possibly succeed.

The distance it takes to travel from that quiet tragedy to transform into triumph is not far at all; it is a distance of inches, millimeters, through a fog of distress that holds us in its grip, yet when it is addressed and confronted turns out to be no more substantial than a bad dream or wisp of fog. ⟩

Maybe you are not where you want to be in life. You may feel blocked, stopped, or held back. Perhaps you have reached a certain level in your relationships, in your career, in your health, in your enjoyment of life, where you have settled.

The good news is *you don't have to settle.*

The Four-Step Process can serve as a doorway to take you through whatever issues or interference patterns have stood in the way of being, doing, and enjoying all that you can imagine. We have seen it happen with thousands of people just like you.

8

A Rich Life

> Hey, I don't have all the answers. In life, to be honest, I
> failed as much as I have succeeded. But I love my wife.
> I love my life. And I wish you my kind of success.
> —Dicky Fox, in *Jerry Maguire*

IN CHAPTER 7 WE talked about people who have used the Four-Step Process to become more productive and effective in their work, and whose incomes have climbed proportionately. But that is only one measure of success. While our culture often equates success with financial riches, that is not necessarily an accurate equation, in and of itself. Success—genuine, lasting, fulfilling, satisfying success—isn't about *being* rich. It's about living a *rich life*.

Five Pathways to a Rich Life

The Four-Step Process does not operate in a vacuum: there are also significant aspects of how we live every day that we can change in order to create the kind of life we truly want.

Over our years of practice, in addition to using and teaching the specific tools of the Four-Step Process, we have developed a number of lifestyle recommendations we make for our clients, stemming in part from the latest in cutting-edge research and in part from our clinical experience. In this final chapter, we wanted to share the essence of these recommendations with you, too.

These are things you can do in addition to the Four-Step Process to help ensure that you live the richest, fullest, and most satisfying life you can. We call these *Five Pathways to a rich life.*

1. Eat consciously.
2. Exercise sanely.
3. Wrap yourself in fractals.
4. Build a gratitude list.
5. Make time for renewal.

Pathway 1: Eat Consciously √

The last few decades of the twentieth century saw a revolution in awareness about food's impact on health. Starting with the landmark 1977 report *Dietary Goals for the United States,* a spate of governmental and private studies dramatically raised both public and professional awareness of the powerful link between nutrition and chronic diseases, such as cardiovascular disease, diabetes, and some forms of cancer.

Today we are in the second wave of that revolution, as we gain a clearer picture of the impact of food on our mental, emotional, and psychological health.

For example, a series of studies during the 1990s demonstrated a clear link between omega-3 and omega-6 fatty acids and cardiovascular health. Research showed that Greenland Eskimos eating their traditional diet of fish, whale, and seal (high in these essential fatty acids—EFAs) had extremely low levels of heart disease and excellent HDL/LDL and cholesterol profiles, and that the fish-eating inhabitants of the typical Japanese fishing village had far lower rates of heart disease and arterial plaque than residents of a similar but non-fish-eating farming village.

But the findings didn't stop there. Researchers soon noticed that the incidence of depression closely followed the same demographic profile: for example, in populations where fish consumption was high, depression was as much as ten times lower than in the United States.

A study at the National Institute on Alcohol Abuse and Alcoholism in Bethesda, Maryland, found a striking reverse correlation between fish consumption and postpartum depression. "Across the board," the study reported, "nations with high levels of fish consumption (Japan, Hong Kong, Sweden, and Chile) had the lowest levels of postpartum depression, and nations with low levels of fish consumption (Brazil, South Africa, West Germany, Saudi Arabia) had the highest rates of postpartum depression."

There is considerable evidence that supplementing the diet with high-quality sources of balanced EFAs may have a significant positive impact on depression and on stabilizing overall mood.

The link between EFAs and mood is just one example; there are others. For instance, there are well-established links between mood and a number of vitamins and minerals that tend to be more abundant in a diet richer in vegetables and fruits and fewer refined foods. In fact, there is a tremendous amount of valuable information available today on the connection of food and mood, and it is not our purpose here to explore it in any detail. The point we make with our clients is simply this: pay attention to what and how you eat, because it makes a difference in how you think and feel. In a phrase, *eat consciously*.

One of the most interesting long-term studies on real-world dietary practice is the National Weight Control Registry (NWCR). In 1994, Rena Wing, Ph.D., from Brown Medical School, and James O. Hill, Ph.D., from the University of Colorado, began recruiting people to participate in an investigation of the patterns and habits of those who had not only lost a significant amount of weight but who had also kept it off. In order to enroll in the registry, you had to have lost at least thirty pounds, as documented by a health professional, and you had to have maintained that lower weight for at least a year's time. In other words, the researchers were looking to see what factors contribute not just to weight *loss*, but to healthy weight *stabilization*.

Starting with about seven hundred adults, the registry grew to the point where today it tracks more than five thousand people. With weight reductions ranging from thirty to three hundred pounds, the average registry participant has lost sixty-six pounds and kept it off for an average of five and a half years. The participants have used a wide variety of approaches to their weight loss and maintenance. However, there are some striking features in common.

For example, 78 percent of NWCR participants eat breakfast every day—not a quick donut and coffee, not a gulped orange juice, but a real breakfast.

Perhaps when you were young, your mother told you the same thing that millions of mothers have told millions of children: "Breakfast is the most important meal of the day." If she did, she was right. Eating a meal with a balance of protein and carbohydrates at the start of the day helps to set a stable pattern for the metabolism throughout the day.

Grabbing a high-sugar snack may give you quick energy, but it does so by generating a rapid spike in blood sugar, typically followed by a precipitous *drop* in blood sugar that can easily throw off your mood, causing irritability, poor concentration, and so forth.

This is true throughout the day. When we wait a long time before eating, often the result is that we have very low blood sugar by the time we do finally eat. ("I'm starving!" we say, even though we are likely nowhere close to literal starvation.) This makes it far more likely that we will then eat a good deal more than we really need, creating a burden on our digestive system and a whole new spike in blood sugar, leading before long to *another* precipitous drop in blood sugar, and around and around the cycle goes—until we crash.

Current nutritional wisdom is that nourishing yourself modestly on nutritious, healthy food five or six times a day tends to keeps your blood sugar regulated so you don't have those fluctuations that pull your mood all over the map.

Another interesting finding at the National Weight Control Registry was that the participants exhibited a *consciously structured* approach to eating. In other words, they had a fairly well-established and carefully thought-out menu and eating pattern. They brought shopping lists when they went food shopping and did not do a lot of impulse buying, nor did they do a lot of impulse eating. In other words, while there was a good deal of variety in their diets, they were consistently *intentional* about what they ate and when they ate it.

Pathway 2: Exercise Sanely

Another common factor in the National Weight Control Registry participants' success, not surprisingly, is *exercise.* Nine out of ten participants exercise, on average, about one hour per day, and 94 percent increased their level of physical activity as part of their approach to achieving and maintaining a healthier weight.

As our modern lifestyle has grown increasingly sedentary, there has been growing interest in targeted physical activities to compensate for the lack of regular exercise. Prior to the 1970s, the idea of everyday citizens (that is, nonathletes) going outside to run, just for the sake of running, was considered, well, weird. Then came the jogging craze, and people have been running ever since. Gym memberships, Pilates and yoga classes, martial arts, home gyms . . . the diversity of ways we have developed to replace the loss of normal physical exertion in our lives is a testament to human ingenuity.

As it turns out, moderate exercise is not only good for the body, it is also good for the mind and mood.

In a study conducted at Duke University, a group of patients were given a thirty-minute program of exercise three times a week, which proved "just as effective as drug therapy in relieving the symptoms of major depression" in a matter of days.

The researchers then followed the patients for six months and found that of those who continued to maintain the exercise routine, only 8 percent saw their depression return, while 38 percent of the drug-only group *and 31 percent of the exercise-plus-drug group* relapsed.

This last finding was particularly fascinating, because it means that the subjects who used an antidepressant drug together with exercise were four times *more* likely to relapse than those who used exercise only, with no drugs at all! Asked what could possibly explain this startling finding, the project director, James Blumenthal, postulated, "Patients who exercised [only] may have felt a greater sense of mastery over their condition and gained a greater sense of accomplishment. They may have felt more self-confident and competent because they were able to do it themselves. . . ."

In a word: the subjects who treated their depression themselves, purely by exercising, had the opportunity to practice greater *self-efficacy*. The fact that they felt they could directly affect their own health could itself have had a beneficial effect on their health.

The benefits of regular moderate exercise don't stop at depression. Mild exercise has also been shown to improve brain functioning in the elderly and may even serve to protect against the advance of Alzheimer's disease.

A recent study showed that simply taking a good walk several times a week can have a profound impact on the physical size of the hippocampus, a fairly tiny, seahorse-shaped structure lying deep within the brain (*hippocampus* is the Latin word for "seahorse") that plays a significant role in the formation of memories.

The hippocampus is especially vulnerable to the impact of trauma. For example, researchers have found that combat veterans and victims of sexual abuse who suffer pronounced post-traumatic stress syndrome also have an unusually small hippocampus, and the smallest hippocampus size correlates with the most severe experience of trauma.

The hippocampus is also one of the first regions of the brain to show signs of deterioration in the progress of Alzheimer's disease. Even in healthy people, this part of the brain typically begins to atrophy about the age of fifty-five or sixty and may shrink as much as 15 percent. But in those suffering with Alzheimer's, the hippocampus will atrophy from 20 percent to 50 percent more than usual.

In early 2011, researchers at the University of Pittsburgh randomly assigned 120 healthy but sedentary men and women averaging sixty years of age to two exercise groups. For the following year, one group did a mild routine including yoga and resistance training with elastic bands. The other group walked around a track three times a week, building up to forty minutes at a stretch.

At the end of the year, brain scans showed that among the yoga-and-resistance-training group, the hippocampus had decreased in size by about 1.4 percent on average. This was no big surprise: such a decrease is considered normal for members of that age group. Among the group who took regular walks, however, the average hippocampus had *increased* in size by about 2 percent—a significant change, especially considering that the hippocampus in these subjects was expected to have *shrunk*, not *grown*.

The interesting thing about exercise is that, as with diet, the guiding principle seems to be balance and moderation. Despite their many benefits, many forms of high-impact activity, including running and most sports, can have a negative effect on the body over the long haul. In many ways, the simplest and most universal exercise is also the most balanced and, in the long term, most beneficial: taking a walk.

The benefits of walking are almost too numerous to fully catalogue. It provides mild cardiovascular benefit. For those in midlife and older, the weight-bearing nature of the activity promotes the absorption of calcium and therefore helps to slow bone loss. Especially in its brisker form, where there is significantly increased respiration and a pronounced swinging of the arms, you have a natural corrective for the biofield's electrical polarity.

What do you suppose the National Weight Control Registry found was the most common form of physical activity among their participants? You guessed it: walking.

Pathway 3: Wrap Yourself in Fractals

Another benefit of taking regular walks is that it puts you in consistent contact with nature—and this has a decidedly positive impact on the nervous system. For decades, longevity studies have associated healthy and relatively stress-free lives with regular contact with a natural environment.

This probably comes as no surprise. After all, it's common sense: being out in nature makes you feel calm and peaceful. But why? As it turns out, there is a science to what nature does, and it is called *fractals*.

Fractals are patterns that repeat themselves at increasing levels of magnification, the recurring, "irregularly repetitive" patterns so often found in nature: clouds, ocean waves, leaves, flowers, and snowflakes. What distinguishes fractals is that they are internally organized with a sort of fuzzy logic through which they repeat themselves but never in precisely identical ways. Thus, no two snowflakes are alike, and you can stare at the clouds or the trees for hours and never see the exact same pattern twice.

Since their discovery in the 1970s by the mathematician Benoit Mandelbrot, fractals have proved enormously helpful in quantifying the complex structure exhibited by a vast range of naturally occurring patterns, in everything from seismology and soil mechanics to human physiology and neurology. They have also captured the imagination of artists as well as scientists and the public at large and have often been referred to as "fingerprints of nature."

Research by Richard Taylor, Ph.D., at the University of Oregon, has shown that the "drip" artwork of Jackson Pollack consists of fractal patterns. We also suspect (though this is not backed up by any research we know of thus far) that the same is true of certain types of modern classical music, such as that by Philip Glass or the Estonian composer Arvo Pärt. For that matter, that familiar fractal effect of the repetition and gradual transformation of small "cells" is the hallmark of much of the music of Bach.

There has also been a considerable amount of research into the impact of fractals on our mood and nervous function. For example, studies have shown that the act of observing fractal patterns—whether occurring in nature, generated mathematically, or as found in artistic expression—generates a distinct electroencephalographic (EEG) pattern in people that includes increased production of alpha waves in the frontal lobe and beta waves in the parietal lobes and has a measurable calming impact on our physiology as measured by skin conductance.

One reason for the psychological and emotional impact of fractals may be that the brain itself is organized in fractal patterns, as a team of researchers at the University of Cambridge has recently shown—a discovery that has helped further our understanding of how the brain works.

Whatever the precise mechanisms involved, the bottom line is this: immersing yourself in fractal environments—such as taking walks out among the trees, grass, clouds, and other natural scenery—has a cooling, calming effect on the limbic system and is tonic for the prefrontal cortex. And this is not a purely visual phenomenon: the sounds and smells of nature, such as birdsong and the mix of scents that surrounds you when you are out among the foliage, and even the feel against your skin of the endlessly fluctuating air currents of nature all these are fractal environments that are balm to the brain.

This effect does not have to stop when you come back indoors, either. For example, in our offices we have pictures and wallpaper depicting beautiful forest scenes. Even when we are not looking at them directly, simply having these fractal patterns in our peripheral vision has a constant soothing effect on the mind and mood. On the aural level, we have a water fountain in our outer office that naturally generates a soft "babbling brook" sound pattern, and through the sound system in our inner offices, a library of CDs quietly plays a fractal symphony of surf and ocean waves in the background.

Pathway 4: Build a Gratitude List

In 2003, two researchers, Robert Emmons, Ph.D., at the University of California, Davis, and Michael McCullough, Ph.D., at the University of Miami, conducted a fascinating experiment. They divided about two hundred subjects into three groups, each of which was instructed to keep a different type of weekly journal. The first group simply recorded daily events without evaluating them; the second recorded annoying and difficult events; and the third made lists of things they were grateful for. At the end of ten weeks, the third group reported a higher energy level, more alertness and optimism, better progress toward goals, and better sleep.

"Research suggests that grateful people have more energy and optimism, are less bothered by life's hassles, are more resilient in the face of stress, have better health, and suffer less depression than the rest of us," writes Joan Borysenko, Ph.D. "People who practice gratitude—and yes, it is something one can learn and improve—are also more compassionate, more likely to help others, less materialistic, and more satisfied with life."

We agree, and we have for years been recommending to our clients a daily practice not unlike what Drs. Emmons and McCullough did with their third group.

Many of us, no matter how positive an outlook we try to maintain, have a tendency to keep our eye out for the negative, to be on alert for what's wrong in our lives rather than what's right. This is not simply a pessimistic attitude; to an extent, we are biologically predisposed to look for what is wrong, what is dangerous, what is harmful, and what is *not working* in our lives. For thousands of years, this was a smart strategy from the standpoint of the survival of the species. If something in our environment was out of the ordinary, it was more likely to kill us.

In today's world, where we do not typically have to fight for survival day in and day out, this predisposition to notice the negative no longer serves us so well. In fact, it is often the force that most strongly limits our potential for living a rich life—because to a great extent, life is a self-fulfilling prophecy: what you focus on is what you get.

Here is how our recommended daily practice works:

Make a list of things you are grateful for, starting with the largest and most obvious. These basic blessings are often things we take for granted, such as:

I am grateful:

. . . that I can see.

. . . that I can walk.

. . . that I have food to eat.

. . . for the sunshine, the air, and the trees.

. . . that I have a car.

. . . that I have a roof over my head.

. . . that I have a friend I trust, spouse I love, and so forth.

We suggest you start by building a list of between one dozen and two dozen items.

Then, choose a time of the day (ideally, about the same time every day) when you can tick through this list mentally, item by item. We have clients who do this in the shower every day, others who make it part of their bedtime ritual, and still others who steal away for a few minutes during lunch hour to step outside the frantic pace of work and ground themselves in a moment of calm reflection.

Once you have this basic list and a time routine established for walking through it every day, here is the rest of the exercise: At least once a day, take out your list, scan through it, and *add one more brand-new item*. Do this every day for the next year, and you will have a list of nearly four hundred things you are grateful for.

There is something very powerful about this: in the process, you will profoundly *change your brain*. Spending this focused time every day on becoming consciously appreciative of a steadily enlarging list of blessings in your life is something like exercising a muscle. You can think of it as *a workout for your gratitude muscle.* And this is not purely a figure of speech. Neurologically speaking, what you are doing through this exercise is retraining a portion of your brain called the *reticular activating system.*

At every moment of every day, we are bombarded by a vast amount of sensory information, data which, if we were to think about it all consciously, would overwhelm us. In order to be able to function, our nervous system filters out all but a very tiny sliver of that information. The reticular activating system is the part of the brain that manages that selection and filtering process.

Also called *reticular formation,* the reticular activating system (RAS) is a network of nerve pathways that connects the brain stem and other lower parts of the brain with the cerebral cortex and cerebellum. This matrix of nerve fibers manages the transition from sleep to wakefulness and vice versa and also acts as a filter for all the sensory input your brain draws from the external world. Everything you see, hear, feel, taste, or smell passes through this fine network, which then relays the signal or message on to the appropriate part of your brain for processing.

The RAS has been described as a "Google of the brain," a search engine that we literally program to pick relevant and useful bits of data out of the vast torrent of sensory information available to us. For example, this is what enables a parent standing outside a crowded gym to pick the sound of her own child out of the undifferentiated stream of sound coming from fifty children inside the building: she has programmed her reticular formation to filter out all the other sounds as irrelevant.

As you build your gratitude list, your RAS makes a subtle shift in its hierarchy of priorities. Rather than looking for what's wrong, you are programming your neural search engine to look for what's *right.* What is going well in your life? What's working for you? As you tick through your list every day, your RAS starts bringing into your awareness those things in your environment and circumstances that conform to what you've made important.

And, just as with the third group in Emmons and McCullough's experiment, as you focus more of your attention on the blessings in your life, they also start to *increase* in your life. That which you focus on, you get more of. As the character Pindar says in the book *The Go-Giver:*

> You've heard the expression, "Go looking for trouble and that's what you'll find"? It's true, and not only about trouble. It's true about *everything*. Go looking for conflict, and you'll find it. Go looking for people to take advantage of you, and they generally will. See the world as a dog-eat-dog place, and you'll always find a bigger dog looking at you as if you're his next meal. Go looking for the best in people, and you'll be amazed at how much talent, ingenuity, empathy and good will you'll find. Ultimately, the world treats you more or less the way you expect to be treated. In fact, you'd be amazed at just how much *you* have to do with what happens to you.

In explaining the concept of the gratitude list to clients, we often describe the case of a gentleman named W. Mitchell.

Mitchell went through a freak motorcycle accident that burned off parts of his fingers and left two-thirds of his body surface covered in severe burns. Several years later a second life-threatening accident (this one in a small plane) left him wheelchair bound. Today he travels the world, giving speeches on overcoming limitations, often speaking for free to groups in prisons and inner-city schools.

"Before I was paralyzed," says Mitchell, "there were ten thousand things I could do. Now there are nine thousand. I could dwell on the one thousand I've lost—or on the nine thousand I have left." This is someone who knows how to manage his own reticular activating system—and has an extremely well-developed gratitude muscle.

Pathway 5: Make Time for Renewal 🅟

In today's fast-paced life, there is often an especially high premium placed on productivity. And make no mistake, being productive is a wonderful thing. But too often, we turn René Descartes's famous dictum, "I think, therefore I am," into its modern, achievement-obsessed version: I *accomplish*, therefore I am.

As we said in chapter 6, balance is the essential element that underlies all the aims of the Four-Step Process, and this is nowhere more true than in the need to balance productive activity with time to refresh, restore, and renew yourself.

Renewal time can mean different things for different people. We look at renewal time in terms of four aspects:

1. Physical renewal
2. Mental renewal
3. Emotional renewal
4. Spiritual renewal

Physical renewal includes getting good sleep as well as good nutrition and good exercise. For so many of us, who normally work in relatively sedentary situations in which we are focused mostly in our minds, simply getting out and moving in the outdoors is often a major source of physical balance.

Mental renewal means doing something that clears your mind and relaxes you mentally. This certainly can include meditation, but it can also simply mean doing something that has nothing to do with all the things you normally do. For example, if your work is in engineering, then reading romance novels or biographies can completely take you away from your normal, everyday focus. Whatever you do as "work," see if you can find something you genuinely enjoy that is wholly unrelated and utterly unlike that area.

Emotional renewal typically means spending time with people you enjoy and who have a renewing effect on you, whether family and close friends or people in your community.

Relationships are, in a sense, living entities unto themselves. They do better when they are maintained and lovingly attended to; they can wither and even die when left alone for too long. We have known people who put more consistent care and attention into changing the oil and spark plugs in their cars than they did on renewing the spark in their key relationships.

And by the way, in terms of emotional renewal time, the definition of *people* needn't be limited solely to human companions. Pets can be, and increasingly are, a source of meaningful emotional renewal, too.

Spiritual renewal varies from person to person, but regardless of your personal religious or faith-related beliefs, we believe spiritual renewal is a crucial aspect of balance for everyone.

If you have a specific faith or spiritual belief system, then this may mean taking time regularly to connect with that faith tradition, whether this means physically going to a place of worship or spending time alone in your home to reconnect with your source. For many people, simply spending time in nature can be a way of reconnecting with that reality that is larger than ourselves—sitting out at night and looking at the stars, taking a walk among the trees, or hiking through the mountains. Whatever it is, the key here is that you make time for it regularly. How often? It's something like physical exercise: it's good to spend at least *some* time within this element daily, and some *significant* time at least several times a week.

As we said in chapter 2, when we feel that connection—to God, to nature, to the larger family of humanity, to life itself—it not only changes our outlook on life, it also changes our physical and psychological health. It gives our life more meaning and makes the experience of our life richer. As a consequence, we live *more* of it.

Rediscovering Our Connection

In the largest sense, all ill health and unhappiness is about disconnection, and health and happiness is about connection. This is ultimately the purpose of the Four-Step Process and the Five Pathways: to help clear away the barriers and impediments to experiencing a full sense of connection—with your true self, with others, and with life.

So many of our problems are exacerbated by the sense that we're alone in the world. When we deeply realize that we are not, that we are each truly an integral, connected part of a larger whole, it begins to have an extraordinarily strong healing effect on every aspect of our lives.

Our colleague Larry Dossey, M.D., the prolific writer on spirituality and medicine, is perhaps best known for his exploration of the power of intercessory prayer in physical healing. In his book *Reinventing Medicine*, Dr. Dossey describes what he sees as three consecutive eras of medicine: Era I medicine, dealing with the physical body; Era II medicine, which encompasses the mind-body model and such approaches as energy psychology; and Era III medicine, which he also terms "eternity medicine," in which patients are affected from a distance through intercessory prayer. Larry told us recently:

I think the larger message of all these remote healing studies is that we *are* connected. When you look at these studies, space and time don't seem to matter. They are one of the great examples we have that we are all part of a nonlocal, universal mind that transcends separation and distance, in space and in time.

In his books, *What Is Life? Mind and Matter* and *My View of the World*, the physicist and Nobel laureate Erwin Schrödinger wrote about what he calls the unitary nature of consciousness, and he says something wonderful: "The overall number of minds is just one." Schrödinger called this the One mind: the idea that we are all part of a greater consciousness that transcends and overcomes individuality and separation. And this is not a saffron-robed Oriental mystic talking this way—this is one of the greatest scientific minds of the twentieth century.

Dr. Candace Pert, the expert on neuropeptides and emotions, puts it this way: "We are hardwired to connect to bliss." This observation forms the theme of her 2007 book *Everything You Need to Know to Feel Go(o)d*.

"But for us to be successful and healthy," she adds, "we have to clear old traumas, so that we can send out clear electronic signals to the universe."

We are not isolated. When we show a kindness to others, it in some small way makes the world a better place—but that also has a healing impact on us, too, as we begin to see ourselves with kinder eyes.

And it works the other way as well. Dissipating the fog of distress and unleashing the truly joyful *you* inside is something you do because it makes *you* feel better. It changes your biochemistry, changes your biofield, changes your moods and thoughts and beliefs, and changes your life. But it also changes those around you, because you are part of them, and they are part of you.

As we heal ourselves, we also heal the world around us. Your personal code to joy is also the path to a more joyful world.

A Deeper Joy

Here comes the sun.
—George Harrison

AS WE SAID IN the introduction, our clinical experiences over the past few decades have shown us that it *is* possible to live happy and fulfilled lives, to experience the full richness of love, connection, and joy that we are capable of. You *can* become a better, smarter, calmer, more focused, more powerful, and more deeply joyful *you*.

For just a moment, though, let's take a closer look at that word, *joy*, and ask what it is we are really talking about here.

The ancient Greeks had two words that could both be translated as "joy": *hedonia*, which is associated with the more immediate pleasures of the moment, and *eudaimonia*, which refers to the pleasure associated with living life in a full and deeply satisfying way.

"The pleasure that comes with, say, a good meal, an entertaining movie or an important win for one's sports team—a feeling called *hedonic well-being*—tends to be short-term and fleeting," as a recent *Wall Street Journal* article entitled "Is Happiness Overrated?" described the distinction. "Raising children, volunteering, or going to medical school may be less pleasurable day to day. But these pursuits give a sense of fulfillment, of being the best one can be, particularly in the long run."

Current research on happiness and well-being often distinguishes between these two sets of values, the hedonistic happiness of short-term gratification and the eudaimonic joy of long-term fulfillment. While these two are not necessarily mutually exclusive—it is certainly possible to live a fulfilling life in pursuit of worthy goals and still enjoy a nice dinner and a movie—they do represent distinctly different types of goals.

There is today a burgeoning field called *positive psychology*, which focuses its efforts on discerning what makes people thrive and live fulfilling lives, as opposed to homing in on the diagnosis and treatment of mental illness. Research in this field has demonstrated that people who focus on living with a eudaimonic sense of purpose tend to live longer and have better mental health as they age than those who focus on achieving more immediate, hedonic feelings of transitory happiness.

In one study of about seven thousand individuals from middle to old age, participants with greater eudaimonic well-being had lower levels of interleukin-6, an inflammatory marker that is associated with cardiovascular disease, osteoporosis, and Alzheimer's disease.

In another study, this one involving about one thousand subjects averaging about eighty years old, those reporting a greater sense of purpose in life were less than half as likely to develop Alzheimer's disease as those with a lesser sense of purpose in life. The higher-sense-of-purpose group were also less likely to be impaired in everyday functions, such as housekeeping, managing money, and walking up or down stairs than those with less sense of purpose. Over a five-year period, they were 57 percent less likely to die.

An American businessman once sought help from the renowned Carl Jung for his drinking problem. After a year of treatment, he soon relapsed. Returning to Jung's office in Switzerland, he inquired what the doctor thought his odds of recovery were.

"You have the mind of a chronic alcoholic," Jung replied. "With many individuals, the methods which I employ are successful—but I have never been successful with an alcoholic of your description."

Coming from one of the great masters of therapy, this was quite a discouraging thing to hear. Disconsolate, the man asked, "Is there no exception?"

"Yes, there is," the great doctor conceded. "Here and there, once in a while, alcoholics have had what are called *vital spiritual experiences*. To me these occurrences appear to be in the nature of huge emotional displacements and rearrangements. Ideas, emotions, and attitudes which were once the guiding forces of the lives of these men are suddenly cast to one side, and a completely new set of conceptions and motives begin to dominate them."

A completely new set of conceptions and motives begin to dominate them. We love that passage, because it is also a strikingly apt description of the kinds of transformations we have seen among our clients who have used the Four-Step Process, often together with the Five Pathways, not only to *improve* but to *transform* their lives.

Remember Stefanie, the client whom we met in the introduction? She visited our offices recently to update us on the events of her life. In the several years since we had first met, she has gone on to create a new business that she recently sold for a substantial sum and is now busily engaged in starting yet another business. Things in her life, on every level from business to family to her personal health, are going very well. When we told her we were writing a book about the Four-Step Process and wondered if we might use her story, she immediately agreed.

"People need this," she said. "If you two can find a way to put what you've done for me between the covers of a book, then by all means, use my story!"

She paused for a moment, then said, "You remember the question I asked, that first day I came to see you? I asked you, *Why aren't I happy?* And you know, I think I found an answer to that question. I think the truth is I already *was* happy, at least on some level that I couldn't feel. I mean, there was a happy Stefanie in there . . . somewhere. I just couldn't find my way there. Does that make sense?"

It sure does.

When that asteroid struck 65 million years ago, the sun may have been blotted out, but that doesn't mean it wasn't still there. The dinosaurs just couldn't see it or feel it. The same is true of whatever cataclysmic or seismic tremors have happened in your life to create the clouds of dust and debris that may have obscured your path up to this point. They may have covered up the road to genuine joy, but that doesn't mean that road wasn't still there.

We were designed and created to be happy. It's our nature. It just gets covered up by the fog of distress. And once we're able to clear away that dark cloud of debris left by the asteroids, earthquakes, and volcanoes of our past, we can see the clear blue skies above and feel the bright, warming sun that never really left us.

George Pratt, Ph.D.
Peter Lambrou, Ph.D.

The Four-Step Process

Step 1: Identify
Purpose: Identify your strongest self-limiting beliefs.

a. Identify your "asteroid strikes."

- Create a list of past events that you feel may have had a strong negative impact on how you see yourself and your world.

- Go through this list and determine which event seems to you has had the deepest or most significant impact.

b. Identify your strongest self-limiting beliefs.

- Identify your strongest self-limiting beliefs, using the personal belief assessment and seven limiting beliefs from chapter 2.

c. Verify the elements you have identified.

- Use neuromuscular feedback to review both lists and arrive at what you see as the single most pertinent past event and single most prevalent self-limiting belief.

Chapters 1–3

Step 2: Clear
Purpose: Rebalance your body's energy system and prepare it for repatterning.

a. Crosshand breathing (two minutes)

- In a seated position, cross your left ankle over your right.

- Place your left hand across your chest, so that the fingers rest over the right side of your collarbone. Then cross your right hand over your left, so that the fingers of your right hand rest over the left side of your collarbone.

- Breathe in through your nose and out through your mouth. As you breathe in, let your tongue touch the roof of your mouth, just behind your front teeth. As you breathe out again, let your tongue rest behind your lower front teeth. You may close your eyes or look down toward the floor to reduce visual stimuli.

b. Grounding (one minute)

- Sit straight and relaxed. Place both hands, one on top of the other, over your solar plexus, just below the bottom of your rib cage. Feel your breath in your belly, slowly rising and falling.

- Now close your eyes, and visualize a cable extending down from your body straight down into the earth.

- Hold that image, breathing slowly in and out, for about one minute.

c. Optional methods

- Use neuromuscular feedback to check your biofield's polarity.

- For persistent or chronic reversal or disorganization, you may also use:

    Cross crawl (two minutes)

    Diamond gait (at least ten minutes)

    Alternate nostril breathing (ten cycles in both directions, about two or three minutes)

Chapter 4

Step 3: Repattern

Purpose: Release negative beliefs and install new empowering beliefs in their place.

a. Healing basket (three minutes)

- Visualize a healing basket or other container of your choosing.

- Place into it all the negative elements from step 1.

- Over the next three minutes or so, visualize it gradually disappearing or floating away, taking all those negative elements with it.

b. Pledge of acceptance (about one minute)

- Place your right hand over your heart and with the tips of your fingers, locate the repatterning spot (between second and third ribs).

- While rubbing this spot in a clockwise motion, repeat your personal code to joy—a statement of self-acceptance plus your self-empowering belief—aloud or silently, five times.

c. Images from your ideal life (several minutes)

- For the next few minutes, visualize scenes and impressions from your empowered, joyful life.

d. Options

- Images of release

- Images of healing journey

- Locate the feeling (energy centers)

- Name and directly address your executive function

- Images of adulthood

Chapter 5

Step 4: Anchor

Purpose: Ensure that the results of the first three steps will be deep and long-lasting.

a. Anchoring hold

- Continue scenes from your ideal life (from step 3) and apply anchoring hold (one minute).

- Continue anchoring hold alone, mind blank, just focused on breathing (one minute).

b. Symbol of balance

- While continuing anchoring hold, now visualize personal symbol of balance (one minute).

Additional Daily Tools

Daily Refresher

Several times daily, for the next thirty days (or as long as you like)

a. Crosshand breathing (two minutes)

b. Pledge and personal code to joy statement, aloud or silent (five times)

c. Anchoring hold, visualizing your personal symbol of balance (one minute)

Mini-Refresher

Anytime you feel stressed and need to reconnect

- Anchoring hold, visualizing your personal symbol of balance (one minute)

Crosshand Breathing

Anytime you feel distressed or that your polarity is out of balance, simply practice two or three minutes of crosshand breathing.

Chapter 6

Five Pathways to a Rich Life

1. Eat consciously.
2. Exercise sanely.
3. Wrap yourself in fractals.
4. Build a gratitude list.
5. Make time for renewal.

Chapter 8

Embracing the Biofield

ALTHOUGH THE CONCEPT OF a subtle energy field organizing and influencing the human body is far from new, it has been only in the past several decades that modern medical science has fully embraced the idea in both theoretical and clinical practice. In fact, for most of the twentieth century the entire notion of a biofield was largely held in ridicule, continuing a long-standing tradition that reached deep into the nineteenth century, when all such research was invariably associated with the auras, séances, and other trappings of the nineteenth-century spiritualism movement.

In the 1840s, the distinguished chemist and geologist Karl Ludwig von Reichenbach worked with a handful of subjects who seemed to be able to detect some kind of human magnetic field, which he dubbed "Odic force." A contemporary of Reichenbach's ascribed the subjects' perceptions to hypnotic suggestion, and his work was quickly discounted.

A half-century later, while working with the newly developed X-ray machine and experimenting with a special blue filter, the British physician Walter Kilner observed an unusual radiation around living subjects. In an effort to disassociate his discovery from the tainted term *aura,* Kilner called this field a "human atmosphere." In 1911, Kilner published his work in a book entitled *The Human Atmosphere*. The following year the *British Medical Journal* lambasted his work, saying, "Dr. Kilner has failed to convince us that his aura is any more real than Macbeth's visionary dagger."

Ouch.

Skeptics notwithstanding, the discoveries kept coming. In the twentieth century, central among these was the work of a dogged researcher who conducted his unconventional work, ironically, at one of the nation's most respected medical colleges. Harold Saxton Burr, M.D., served on the faculty at Yale University for nearly fifty years during the first half of the twentieth century. Along with his duties teaching conventional anatomy, Professor Burr also dedicated thousands of hours to research, publishing nearly one hundred scientific papers. He is best known for his discovery that all living organisms, both plant and animal, are shaped and influenced by distinct electromagnetic (EM) fields that could be measured and mapped using sensitive voltmeters.

Dr. Burr's hypothesis was that this EM field maintained the essential identity of the organism: much as iron filings scattered on a piece of paper will assume the shape of a magnet held underneath the paper, the nutritive elements in our bloodstream and other products of metabolism take the "shape" of our organism as dictated by its underlying biofield.

In the 1940s, the Russian electrician and inventor Semyon Kirlian developed an extremely sensitive camera apparatus that captured images of these biofields in the form of high-voltage, high-frequency electronic cycles. First gaining widespread recognition in the early 1960s, Kirlian photographs revealed a compelling pattern of electron energy radiation taking the form of an aura enveloping the organism, much like Earth's magnetosphere, which had only recently been discovered. (Interestingly, the magnetosphere bears a striking resemblance to the human form.)

At the same time that Kirlian's photographic evidence was becoming known in the West, an American orthopedic surgeon named Robert O. Becker, M.D., was investigating the possible relationship of electrical properties of the body with the healing of fractures. Why was it, he wondered, that a newt or salamander could regenerate a lost limb, but a human could not?

Dr. Becker soon discovered an interesting phenomenon. The electrical polarity at the end of the severed nerve in the limb of a salamander is opposite that of higher organisms, such as dogs, cats, or humans. Might this play a role in why certain species (like salamanders) are able to regenerate limbs, and others (like humans) are not? And if you changed the electrical polarity at the end of a human nerve, could you possibly stimulate new growth there?

As it turned out, you could. Dr. Becker's findings led to the development of the electronic bone growth stimulator (EBGS), a tool that is used today in orthopedic medicine to assist in severe breaks from which the bones would not otherwise be able to regenerate properly, such as fractures in very large bones like the femur, or in cases where the damage has been left too long for normal healing to take place. The EBGS has also been tested as effective in speeding the healing of vertebrae fusions and back pain.

An epic milestone in the story of energy medicine occurred in 1971, when President Richard Nixon initiated a mission to open up diplomatic ties between China and the West. Six months before the president's historic visit, an advance team arrived in Peking (now Beijing) to begin laying the groundwork, accompanied by a small press corps that included the veteran *New York Times* reporter James Reston.

Several days after his arrival in Peking, Reston began experiencing intense abdominal pain. Within hours he was undergoing an emergency appendectomy at Peking's Anti-Imperialist Hospital. The surgery was successful, but the patient soon began experiencing acute postoperative pain. Much to Reston's astonishment, the treatment consisted solely of two methods: acupuncture and moxabustion—the insertion of needles and burning of aromatic herbs on key acupuncture points. The patient's discomfort vanished; the treatment was completely successful.

A week later, Reston wrote about his experience in the *New York*

Times, and the Western world had its eyes opened to a whole new understanding of how human beings are constructed—and how they may be treated.

The clinical practice of acupuncture, especially (though far from exclusively) for the treatment of pain, soon began to move outside the small circle of Oriental medicine practitioners treating their Asian communities. As its reputation spread, Western practitioners began receiving training as well, and the practice flourished. Today there are tens of thousands of licensed acupuncturists in practice in the United States, with similar numbers everywhere in the Western world.

The scientific community, however, was not so quick to embrace the validity of the core concept behind acupuncture and acupressure. It was not until more than a quarter-century later that acupuncture finally received a stamp of approval from the U.S. government's primary agency for medical research.

In November 1997, the National Institutes of Health convened a twelve-member panel of experts representing a range of fields including biophysics, epidemiology, family practice, internal medicine, physical medicine and rehabilitation, physiology, psychiatry, psychology, public health policy, and statistics. Twenty-five additional experts presented evidence to the panel and a conference audience of twelve hundred. In its report, the panel praised acupuncture for its demonstrated lack of side effects and cited evidence for its efficacy in conditions ranging from postoperative dental pain and nausea from chemotherapy to addiction, arthritis, and stroke rehabilitation.

"Further research," added the report in its conclusion, "is likely to uncover additional areas where acupuncture interventions will be useful."

Perhaps the most promising among these efforts has been the Neuroimaging Acupuncture Effects on Human Brain Activity project at Harvard Medical School (discussed in chapter 4), which published its first paper in 2000 and has been ongoing ever since. Using fMRI and positive emission tomography (PET) scans to show the impact of acupoint stimulation on the brain, the project has shown that key acupoints can cause a calming of the limbic system—the brain's stress-response system, including the amygdala, hippocampus, and others—within seconds of treatment.

Over the past two decades, energy medicine has emerged as one of the most exciting frontiers in medical practice. Today more than one hundred of the nation's premier medical institutions have programs that include some aspect of energy medicine and energy psychology, many of which did not exist at the turn of the new century. For example, following are a dozen prominent medical institutions, listed together with the subsidiaries or departments they have recently created that all employ energy medicine:

1. Beaumont Hospital: *Integrative Medicine*
2. Duke University Medical Center: *Duke Integrative Medicine*
3. Hartford Hospital: *Integrative Medicine Department*
4. Henry Ford Hospital: *Center for Integrative Medicine*
5. New York-Presbyterian Hospital: *Richard and Hinda Rosenthal Center for Complementary and Alternative Medicine*
6. Ohio State University Medical Center: *Center for Integrative Medicine*
7. Scripps Clinic: *Center for Integrative Medicine*
8. Stanford Hospital and Clinic: *Stanford Center for Integrative Medicine*
9. Thomas Jefferson University: *Myrna Brind Center of Integrative Medicine*
10. University of Colorado: *Center for Integrative Medicine*
11. University of Texas: *M.D. Anderson Cancer Center's Complementary/Integrative Medicine Education Resources*
12. Yale University: *Griffin Hospital's Integrative Medicine Center*

These top institutions and dozens of others like them use various energy medicine methodologies, for example, in their approaches to cardiac, surgical, and postoperative care, and are increasingly exploring their application to conditions of mood and mind, such as anxiety, depression, and post-traumatic stress disorder.

It's hard to grasp why there should have been so much resistance to this direction in medicine because, despite the decades of controversy, there is nothing radical about the idea that human beings are electrical in nature.

For example, when doctors want to assess the health of your heart, they might run an electrocardiogram (EKG). Why? Because they can see the relative health of the heart's function by reading a chart of its electrical output. Likewise, we use an electroencephalogram (EEG) to measure your brain's electrical activity, and electromyography (EMG) to measure the electrical activities of the muscles. We also know we need to maintain a certain balance of sodium, potassium, calcium, magnesium, and other electrically charged minerals (ions), called *electrolytes,* in the blood and body tissues. Why? Because the signals in all our nerves are electrical impulses.

In fact, every aspect of the body is electrically managed and oriented; the human being is a fundamentally electrical phenomenon. And embracing this understanding in our approach to healing has provided what turns out to be a crucial missing element in our age-old quest for greater peace of mind, overall well-being, and optimum performance as human beings. It provides, in other words, a linchpin in our capacity to dispel that pervasive fog of distress and become more fully and richly *ourselves.*

NOTES

The following notes are listed by relevant page number and the referenced text excerpt.

Introduction: Stefanie's Question

p. 1: *A woman named Stefanie came to our office seeking treatment.*

In actuality, our clients see one or the other of us for treatment, not both of us together. However, for purposes of simplicity and narrative clarity, we describe clients as coming to see "us" or visiting "our office" throughout this book.

p. 3: *A blanket of fog an acre round and one meter deep.*

In his book *The Essence of Success*, the famed broadcaster and sales trainer Earl Nightingale wrote, "According to the Bureau of Standards, a dense fog covering seven city blocks, to a depth of 100 feet, is composed of something less than one glass of water."

In researching this claim, we consulted with the U.S. National Institute of Standards and Technology (as the Bureau of Standards was renamed in 1988).

It seems most likely that Nightingale was citing a passage from a 1926 publication entitled *Fogs and Clouds*, by W. J. Humphreys for the U.S. Weather Bureau (Williams & Wilkins Co., Baltimore), which in turn cited a 1916 publication of the U.S. Coast Guard, "Report on an Investigation of Fog in the Vicinity of the Grand Banks of Newfoundland, Done Aboard the Ice Patrol Cutter Seneca during the May Cruise of 1915, by the Bureau of Standards," in *Bulletin No. 5, International Ice Observation and Ocean Patrol Service in the North Atlantic Ocean*, Govt. Printing Office, Washington, D.C., 1916.

The 1926 passage in question reads, "A block of fog three feet wide, six feet high, and one hundred feet long contains less than one-seventh of a glass of liquid water. Barely one good swallow!"

Further research corroborated these numbers. Although Nightingale's image was a bit of an exaggeration, the image was so striking that we used it here, redoing the math to make it accurate and amending his "seven city blocks to a depth of 100 feet" to our one acre, one meter deep.

p. 5: *We have spent the past several decades unraveling this puzzle, using the tools of conventional psychology along with new methods and insights from the latest findings at the cutting edge of a field of research and therapy called energy psychology.*

We did not start out on this path. In fact, we both went through wholly conventional training as clinical psychologists, using the standard techniques of our profession, and like any properly trained psychologists, we relied on methodologies that had been taught to us by our professors and were part of the accepted canon of the scientific mainstream.

However, by the late 1980s, when Peter joined George in clinical practice, we shared a sense that there were new frontiers to be explored in our field. We had both encountered and puzzled over many variations of Stefanie's question and had chafed against the limitations of our profession's current accepted norms.

We were not alone. About this time, the traditional mechanistic view of human health was starting to give way to a broader, more multidisciplinary view, and a new direction in medicine was just beginning to emerge. Not everyone thought that the laboratory-pure, stimulus/response model accounted for what was going on in the human organism. This was not a unified or highly organized effort, but a decentralized, grassroots shift taking place in hundreds of different locations and areas of investigation.

Even as we pursued our practice using the normal conventional tools of our profession, we also began searching for possible new avenues of research and modality.

We studied hypnosis (both of us had written on the topic: Peter coauthored *Self-Hypnosis* with Brian Alman in 1983, and George was coauthor with Brian Alman and Dennis Wood of *A Clinical Hypnosis Primer* in 1984), eye movement desensitization and reprocessing (EMDR) and neuro-linguistic programming (NLP), biofeedback, guided imagery, Gestalt, and many other intriguing avenues of exploration, in some cases even going so far as to work with the founders of those unconventional and intriguing methodologies. Some were more effective than others, and all had something to contribute—but none quite showed us the path over the mountains.

A major milestone for us came in 1995, when we learned about the possibilities of using an intriguing, wholly noninvasive diagnostic process called *behavioral kinesiology* or *muscle testing*, which we refer to as *neuromuscular feedback*, from a friend and colleague, Dr. Greg Nicosia. Greg employed this method to draw a vast scope and depth of information from his subjects. The data he mined ranged from subject's eating habits and health histories to family dynamics and all sorts of other psychological issues. The degree of detail his simple demonstrations extracted from his subjects (including ourselves) was staggering.

We explore neuromuscular feedback in some depth in chapter 3.

Chapter 1: An Interview with Yourself

p. 12: *Bessel van der Kolk, M.D., perhaps the world's leading authority on trauma, describes the amygdalae as "the smoke detector of the brain."*

From a private conversation with the authors.

Chapter 2: Seven Limiting Beliefs

p. 35: *With advanced methods of brain imaging, and especially functional magnetic resonance imaging (fMRI), scientists in the past two decades have gained an astonishing ability to peer into the physical workings of the brain.*

Magnetic resonance imaging (MRI) was a great advance over computed tomography (CT) scans, which showed hard tissue, because MRI could image soft tissue—discs, and so on, as well as brain tissue—by showing tissue that was consuming oxygen. In other words, CT scans were more anatomical and structural, while the newer imaging techniques had more potential to show what was functionally happening inside the body.

Then came the *functional* MRI, or fMRI, a special type of MRI that measures changes in neural activity through changes in blood flow and blood oxygen levels in the brain or spinal cord. The principle behind the process was developed in 1990 and first implemented in experimental form in 1991. It was rapidly adopted for widespread use in both diagnosis and research. In part because it does not involve the use of radioactive dyes, as other forms of scans do (CT and PET), it can be used repeatedly without harm. Since the early 1990s, fMRI has come to dominate the brain-mapping field due to its relatively low invasiveness, absence of radiation exposure, and relatively wide availability.

Positive emission tomography (PET) scans perform similar imaging but require a radioactive isotope, which makes repeated measurements more difficult. It is a more robust diagnostic in some ways but is more limited for research purposes.

As fMRIs have become more powerful (in essence, by using larger magnets), they have been able to measure more detail with ever more precision. Ten or fifteen years from now, who knows: perhaps we'll have personal fMRI devices hooked up to our laptops, digital pads, or cell phones.

p. 69: *"The eternal silence of these infinite spaces terrifies me,"* wrote the seventeenth-century scientist Blaise Pascal.

"Le silence éternel de ces espaces infinis m'effraye," from Pascal's posthumously collected *Pensées and Other Writings.*

Chapter 3: The Flea and the Elephant

p. 81: *"At the end of the [nineteenth] century,"* as Tor Norretrander writes in The User Illusion, *"the notion of the transparent man was severely challenged."*

Norretrander, T. *The User Illusion: Cutting Consciousness Down to Size,* Penguin, 1991, p. 162.

p. 90: *"People have a hard time discriminating between physical and mental pain,"* says Dr. Pert.

From Dr. Pert's website (www.candacepert.com) and private conversations with the authors.

p. 99:*One of the most striking confirmations of neuromuscular feedback appeared more than a decade ago.*

Monti, D. A., et al. "Muscle Test Comparisons of Congruent and Incongruent Self-Referential Statements," *Perceptual and Motor Skills*, 1999, 88, pp. 1019–28.

Chapter 4: A Disturbance in the Force

p. 108: *Chantal was one of fifty Rwandan orphans who participated in the study.*

Chantal is not the girl's real name, but her story and the landmark Rwandan study are very real indeed. The study, authored by Caroline Sakai, Suzanne Connolly, and Paul Oas, was published in 2010 in the *International Journal of Emergency Mental Health*, Winter 2010, 12(1), pp. 41–50, under the title "Treatment of PTSD in Rwandan Child Genocide Survivors Using Thought Field Therapy." Text of the article can be found at www.tftcenter.com/articles_treatment_of_ptsd_rwanda.html.

p. 109: *One study with traumatized adolescents followed sixteen teenage boys in Peru who had all been severely abused.*

Church, D., Piña, O., Reategui, C., & Brooks, A. "Single Session Reduction of the Intensity of Traumatic Memories in Abused Adolescents: A Randomized Controlled Trial." Paper presented at the Eleventh Annual Toronto Energy Psychology Conference, October 15–19, 2009. As of this writing, this study is undergoing peer review at both the *Journal of Child Sexual Abuse* and the journal *Psychological Trauma*.

p. 109: *In a randomized, double-blind pilot study in South America conducted over five and a half years.*

Andrade, J., & Feinstein, D. "Preliminary Report of the First Large-Scale Study of Energy Psychology." Initiated in the late 1980s, this research review included various studies over a fourteen-year period and was published in 2004 as an appendix to David Feinstein's *Energy Psychology Interactive: Rapid Interventions for Lasting Change* (Innersource).

p. 109: *In a randomized, controlled trial with combat veterans.*

Church, D., Hawk, C, Brooks, A., Toukolehto, O., Wren, M., Dinter, I., & Stein, P. "Psychological Trauma in Veterans using EFT (Emotional Freedom Techniques): A Randomized Controlled Trial." These data were presented at the Society of Behavioral Medicine, Seattle, Washington, April 7–10, 2010. As of this writing, the study is undergoing peer review.

A ten-minute clip containing brief excerpts of interviews with four combat veterans before and after energy psychology treatment, along with snippets from the treatments they received, can be found at www.vetcases.com.

p. 110: *For example, one of the therapists in the combat veterans study cited described her work with Keith, an infantry soldier who'd served in the Mekong Delta during the Vietnam War.*

The therapist's name is Ingrid Dinter; her remarks are taken from an interview with Ms. Dinter by David Feinstein, Ph.D., as reported in his article, "The Case for Energy Psychology: Snake Oil or Designer Tool for Neural Change?" *Psychotherapy Networker,* November 2010, www.innersource.net/ep/images/stories/downloads/ PN_article.pdf.

p. 111: *The* biofield *itself, a very fine electromagnetic field that begins at the level of the skin and extends outward for several inches or farther.*

The extent of this field's reach is still a matter of some debate, in part because our ability to determine this is dependent on the instruments used to measure it. Some scientists speculate that our biofields overlap and may extend a virtually infinite distance. What we do presently know is that the biofield is not contained exclusively within the outer surface of the physical body.

Electrical signals from the heart and brain, for example, are not measured directly on either organ (if they were, you would have drill into the skull every time you wanted to take an EEG or crack open the chest for every EKG), but from a distance of at least half an inch and typically more. Certainly the closer to the source the more precise the signal, but if our instruments were more sensitive, we might be able to detect and interpret those signals from several inches, even several feet away.

p. 121: *An ongoing study at Harvard using brain imaging to observe in real time the effects on the brain of acupuncture.*

The Neuroimaging Acupuncture Effects on Human Brain Activity project at Harvard Medical School: www.nmr.mgh.harvard.edu/acupuncture/PPG. (See also Appendix B: Embracing the Biofield.)

p. 122: *"What the Harvard studies have shown . . ."*

From a private conversation with the authors.

p. 122: *" . . . when you stimulate certain acupressure points, this sends a signal to the amygdala that decreases arousal."*

Typically the singular *amygdala* and plural *amygdalae* are used interchangeably, and we have followed that convention here.

p. 123: *For the past several decades, we have used a broad inventory of tools and methodologies in our practice, including methods such as eye movement desensitization and reprocessing (EMDR).*

EMDR is an innovative treatment method pioneered in the late 1980s by Francine Shapiro, Ph.D.

The story of how Dr. Shapiro came to develop the process is interesting. While walking in a park one day, she stopped and stood at a pond's edge for a while to gaze at some ducks while she mulled over some issue she was distressed about. Suddenly she noticed that she had begun to feel inexplicably calmer and more relaxed—and the effect seemed to occur as she moved her eyes back and forth to follow the ducks' movements on the pond's surface.

Careful deconstruction and experimentation of the experience led her to formulate the EMDR process, which proved to be a wonderful tool for resolving posttraumatic stress and other emotional blocks to normal functioning. While the client focuses on the memory of the disturbing experience, the therapist moves her hand (or an object, or a light) from side to side in front of the subject's face. This process somehow allows the subject to "reprocess" the event, creating new associational pathways in the brain and dissolving the emotional blocks.

We began using the method soon after it was created and found that it enabled us to treat effectively a wide range of clients, including some with issues that had failed to yield even to hypnosis. Moreover, the treatment worked in a fraction of the time, often accomplishing in weeks what more traditional therapies would take months to achieve—if they achieved them at all.

One potential drawback with EMDR is that in the course of treatment, it is possible for the subject to be retraumatized, that is, to re-experience some of the impact of the original trauma in a way that does more harm than good. This is not a danger in the hands of a qualified and experienced professional, but it is one reason we do not incorporate this approach in the self-administered model presented here.

p. 123: *And the acupoint tapping used by Caroline Sakai in Rwanda.*

One of our colleagues, Sandra Bagley, Ph.D., a board-certified nurse practitioner who worked for an international humanitarian team, went to the war-ravaged regions of Kosovo after the atrocities in Bosnia and Croatia and used the acupointtapping methods she learned from several of our workshops to help the traumatized survivors there. She also taught the field physicians how to apply some of the basic procedures to help the mentally and physically wounded.

The popular energy psychology methodology of tapping, in fact, served as the basis of our previous book, *Instant Emotional Healing: Acupressure for the Emotions* (Broadway Books, 2000). However, for the present book we wanted to offer a simpler and even more readily accessible approach.

Chapter 5: Your Personal Code to Joy

p. 133: *Our colleague V. S. Ramachandran, M.D., Ph.D., points out in his wonderful book,* The Tell-Tale Brain.

Ramachandran, V. S. *The Tell-Tale Brain: A Scientist's Quest for What Makes Us Human,* Norton, 2011.

p. 133: *"It is as if mirror neurons are nature's own virtual reality simulations of the intentions of other beings."*
     The Tell-Tale Brain, p. 121.

p. 133: *The new understanding of mirror neurons helps to explain an entire body of research, going back for more than a hundred years, that says the images we hold in our minds can have a tangible impact on our behavior and physical abilities.*
     MacIntyre, T. E., & Moran, A. P. "A Qualitative Investigation of Imagery Use and Meta-Imagery Processes Among Elite Canoe-Slalom Competitors." *Journal of Imagery Research in Sports and Physical Activity*, 2007, 2(1), Article 3.

p. 133: *For example, in one oft-cited 1977 study, a group of seventy-two college basketball players was split into four groups.*
     Kolonay, B. J. "The Effects of Visuo-Motor Behavior Rehearsal on Athletic Performance," master's thesis, Hunter College, Department of Psychology, 1977. Kolonay went on to get her doctorate in sports psychology at Tulane University and gained considerable notice for her work on the compatibility of players on NBA teams.

p. 134: *Similar results were found in subsequent studies employing a similar visualization process in such fields as karate, tennis serving, and pistol marksmanship.*
     Onestak, D. M. "The Effect of Visuo-Motor Behavior Rehearsal (VMBR) and Videotaped Modeling on the Free-Throw Performance of Intercollegiate Athletes," *Journal of Sport Behavior*, 1997, 20, www.questia.com/googleScholar qst?docId=5002239520.

p. 135: *Dr. Doidge describes an extraordinary experiment conducted in the early 1990s by Drs. Guang Yue and Kelly Cole.*
     Yue, G., & K. J. Cole. "Strength Increases from the Motor Program: Comparison of Training with Maximal Voluntary and Imagined Muscle Contractions," *Journal of Neurophysiology* 67(5), 1992, pp. 1114–23. Cited in Doidge, N., *The Brain That Changes Itself*, Penguin, 2007, p. 204.

p. 136: *"The life-force may be the least understood force on earth,"* wrote Cousins.
     Cousins, N. *The Anatomy of an Illness as Perceived by the Patient*, Bantam Doubleday Dell, 1981, p. 54.

p. 136: *"Positive thoughts have a profound effect on behavior and genes . . . ,"* writes Dr. Lipton, *"and negative thoughts have an equally powerful effect."*
     Lipton, B. *The Biology of Belief*, Mountain of Love/Elite Books, 2005, p. 30.

p. 137: *The concept and importance of self-efficacy were championed starting in the 1970s by the noted Canadian psychologist Albert Bandura.*

One of the most influential figures in the development of cognitive psychology, Dr. Bandura ranked in a 2002 *Review of General Psychology* survey as the fourth most-often cited psychologist of all time, ranking only behind B. F. Skinner, Jean Piaget, and Sigmund Freud.

Bandura devoted much of his career from the late 1970s onward to exploring the role of self-efficacy in human behavior, publishing work on the topic, *Self-Efficacy: The Exercise of Control,* Worth Publishers, 1997.

p. 138: *[Those with poor self-efficacy] shy away from difficult tasks, which they view as personal threats.*

Bandura, A. "Self-Efficacy," in V. S. Ramachandran (ed.), *Encyclopedia of Human Behavior* (vol. 4, pp. 71–81), Academic Press, 1994.

p. 143: *According to Bessel van der Kolk, M.D., trauma has a particular impact on the posterior cingulate.*

From a private conversation with the authors.

p. 153: *In the intercostal space between the second and third ribs.*

The ribs are numbered counting down from the top. The first rib tucks directly under the clavicle (collarbone). The second rib is generally easier to find than the first, and the third is even more exposed.

p. 153: *Rubbing this spot triggers a neurolymphatic response that functions something like a major acupoint.*

This repatterning spot does not correspond to a specific acupoint but has been found empirically to have a significant impact on the biofield. You can find the same nerve bundle on both sides of the rib cage, but over the years of working with this process, we have found that working with the location on the left side yields better and more consistent results.

Chapter 8: A Rich Life

p. 198: *Starting with the landmark 1977 report* Dietary Goals for the United States.

Sometimes called simply "The McGovern Report," this was a report issued by the U.S. Senate Select Subcommittee on Nutrition and Human Needs.

p. 198: *A series of studies during the 1990s demonstrated a clear link between omega-3 and omega-6 fatty acids and cardiovascular health.*

Stoll, A. L. *The Omega-3 Connection,* Fireside (Simon & Schuster), 2001.

p. 198: *Researchers soon noticed that the incidence of depression closely followed the same demographic profile.*

The Omega-3 Connection, pp. 43–44.

p. 199: *A study at the National Institute on Alcohol Abuse and Alcoholism in Bethesda, Maryland, found a striking reverse correlation between fish consumption and postpartum depression.*

The Omega-3 Connection, pp. 101–2.

p. 201: *In a study conducted at Duke University, a group of patients were given a thirty-minute program of exercise three times a week.*

"Study: Exercise Has Long-Lasting Effect on Depression," press release issued by Duke University, Chapel Hill, NC, September 22, 2000.

p. 202: *A recent study showed that simply taking a good walk several times a week can have a profound impact on the physical size of the hippocampus.*

Span, P. "Fitness: A Walk to Remember? Study Says Yes," *New York Times*, February 7, 2011, www.nytimes.com/2011/02/08/health/research/08fitness.html. The study mentioned in the article is "Exercise Training Increases Size of Hippocampus and Improves Memory," Erik L. Erikson et al., *The Proceedings of the National Academy of Sciences*, February 15, 2011 (published online January 31: www.pnas.org/content/108/7/3017).

p. 202: *The hippocampus is especially vulnerable to the impact of trauma.*

Bower, B. "Exploring Trauma's Cerebral Side," *Science News*, May 18, 1996, 140, p. 315.

p. 204: *Research by Richard Taylor, Ph.D., at the University of Oregon, has shown that the "drip" artwork of Jackson Pollack consists of fractal patterns.*

http://pages.uoregon.edu/msiuo/taylor/art/info.html.

p. 206: *One reason for the psychological and emotional impact of fractals may be that the brain itself is organized in fractal patterns.*

Pincus, D. "Fractal Thoughts on Fractal Brains," *Psychology Today* blog, September 4, 2009: www.psychologytoday.com/blog/the-chaotic-life/200909/fractal-brains-fractal-thoughts. The 2008 Cambridge study Dr. Pincus refers to is "Broadband Criticality of Human Brain Network Synchronization," www.ncbi.nlm.nih.gov/pubmed/19300473?ordinalpos=14&itool=EntrezSystem2.PEntrez.Pubmed.Pubmed_ResultsPanel.Pubmed_DefaultReport.

p. 206: *In 2003, two researchers, Robert Emmons, Ph.D., at the University of California, Davis, and Michael McCullough, Ph.D., at the University of Miami, conducted a fascinating experiment.*

Emmons, R. A., & McCullough, M. E. "Counting Blessings Versus Burdens: An Experimental Investigation of Gratitude and Subjective Well-Being in Daily Life," *Journal of Personality and Social Psychology*, 2003, 84 (2), pp. 377–89. www.chucklin.org/wp-content/uploads/2010/02/Emmons_McCullough_2003_JPSP.pdf.

Dr. Emmons has authored three books on the topic: *The Psychology of Ultimate Concerns* (Guilford Press, 1999), *The Psychology of Gratitude* (Oxford University Press, 2004), and *Thanks!: How the New Science of Gratitude Can Make You Happier* (Houghton Mifflin Harcourt, 2008). See also http://psychology.ucdavis.edu/labs/emmons/PWT/index.cfm.

p. 206: *"Research suggests that grateful people have more energy and optimism."*
Borysenko, J., "Practicing Gratitude: Why Being Thankful Is the Secret to a Happier, Healthier Life," *Prevention*, November 10, 2004, www.prevention.com/health/health/emotional-health/practicing-gratitude/article/0f725d1fa803110VgnVCM10000013281eac_____.

p. 209: *As the character Pindar says in the book* The Go-Giver.
Burg, B., & Mann, J. D. *The Go-Giver*, Portfolio 2007, pp. 15–16.

p. 209: *In explaining the concept of the gratitude list to clients, we often describe the case of a gentleman named W. Mitchell.*
Burrus, D., & Mann, J. D. *Flash Foresight*, HarperBusiness, 2011, p. 222. Also see www.wmitchell.com.

p. 212: *In his book* Reinventing Medicine, *Dr. Dossey describes what he sees as three consecutive eras of medicine.*
Dossey, L. *Reinventing Medicine: Beyond Mind-Body to a New Era in Medicine*, HarperCollins, 1999.

p. 212: *Dr. Candace Pert, the expert on neuropeptides and emotions, puts it this way: "We are hardwired to connect to bliss."*
Remarks from a private conversation with the authors.

Conclusion: A Deeper Joy

p. 215: *"The pleasure that comes with, say, a good meal, an entertaining movie or an important win for one's sports team—a feeling called* hedonic well-being—*tends to be short-term and fleeting," a recent* Wall Street Journal *article entitled "Is Happiness Overrated?" described the distinction.*
Wang, S. S. "Is Happiness Overrated? Study Finds Physical Benefits to Some (Not All) Good Feelings," *Wall Street Journal*, March 15, 2011, http://online.wsj.com/article_email/SB10001424052748704893604576200471545379388-lMyQjAxMTAxMDEwNTExNDUyWj.html.

p. 216: *Current research on happiness and well-being often distinguishes between these two sets of values, the hedonistic . . . and the eudaimonic.*

For example, Edward Deci and Richard Ryan write, "Research on well-being can be thought of as falling into two traditions. In one—the hedonic tradition—the focus is on happiness, generally defined as the presence of positive affect and the absence of negative affect. In the other—the eudaimonic tradition—the focus is on living life in a full and deeply satisfying way." From Deci, E. L., & Ryan, R. M., "Hedonia, Eudaimonia, and Well-Being: An Introduction," *Journal of Happiness Studies*, 2008, 9, pp. 1–11.

p. 216: *In one study of about seven thousand individuals . . . participants with greater eudaimonic well-being had lower levels of interleukin-6.*

Funded by the National Institute on Aging, the study is called MIDUS, or the "Mid-Life in the U.S. National Study of Americans." It has been running since 1995, led by Dr. Carol Ryff, a professor and director of the Institute on Aging at the University of Wisconsin, Madison. You can read about this study, as well as the one that follows, in the excellent *Wall Street Journal* article "Is Happiness Overrated? Study Finds Physical Benefits to Some (Not All) Good Feelings," by Shirley S. Wang.

p. 216: *In another study, this one involving about one thousand subjects . . . those reporting a greater sense of purpose in life were less than half as likely to develop Alzheimer's disease.*

This seven-year study took place at the Alzheimer's Disease Center at Rush University Medical Center in Chicago, led by the center's director, David Bennett. (Reported in Wang, "Is Happiness Overrated?")

p. 216: *An American businessman once sought help from the renowned Carl Jung for his drinking problem.*

Alcoholics Anonymous: The Big Book, 4th ed., 2002, pp. 26–27.

Appendix B: Embracing the Biofield

p. 227: *Dr. Becker soon discovered an interesting phenomenon.*

Robert O. Becker reported his findings in his enormously popular book *The Body Electric* (William Morrow, 1985) and further in his book *Cross Currents: The Promise of Electromedicine, the Perils of Electropollution* (Tarcher, 1989).

p. 227: *Dr. Becker's findings led to the development of the electronic bone growth stimulator (EBGS).*

Kane, W. J. "Direct Current Electrical Bone Growth Stimulation for Spinal Fusion," Department of Orthopaedic Surgery, Northwestern University Medical School, Chicago, Illinois. www.ncbi.nlm.nih.gov/pubmed/3291140.

p. 227: *A week later, Reston wrote about his experience in the* New York Times.

Reston, J., "Now Let Me Tell You About My Appendectomy in Peking," *New York Times*, July 26, 1971, http://select.nytimes.com/gst/abstract.html?res=FB0D11F A395C1A7493C4AB178CD85F458785F9.

p. 228: *In November 1997, the National Institutes of Health convened a twelve-member panel of experts.*

"Acupuncture: NIH Consensus Statement," November 3–5, 1997, 15(5), pp. 1–34. The conference report is available for review at http://consensus.nih.gov/1997/1997 Acupuncture107html.htm.

p. 228: *Perhaps the most promising among these efforts has been the Neuroimaging Acupuncture Effects on Human Brain Activity project at Harvard Medical School, which published its first paper in 2000.*

Hui, K. K., et al. "Acupuncture Modulates the Limbic System and Subcortical Gray Structures of the Human Brain: Evidence from fMRI Studies in Normal Subjects," *Human Brain Mapping*, 2000, 9(1), pp. 13–25. Also see www.nmr.mgh .harvard.edu/acupuncture/PPG/.

ACKNOWLEDGMENTS

THERE ARE MOMENTS IN life when we may fall prey to the illusion that we exist and act in isolation. "*I did that!*" we may think. "That was *me*, all by myself!" Honest reflection quickly reveals that nothing could be further from the truth. From conception through career and the legacies we leave behind, there is nothing that we can truly claim to have accomplished all by ourselves. To breathe is to exchange; to live is to collaborate; and to succeed in making even the smallest of contributions to the world is to have experienced the grace of partnership.

In no act is this truth more evident than in the creation of a book. Writing *Code to Joy* has been an absolute delight at every step, from the earliest impulse to the finalizing details, and to say "We couldn't have done it alone" seems an understatement of ludicrous proportions.

This may not be common protocol, but the first acknowledgment we need to give voice to is a moment of thanks and appreciation to each other.

It is a rare treasure to have both a professional relationship and a friendship that builds and grows ever stronger over nearly three decades. Both of us are blessed to have experienced this rare treasure with each other. This book (like our previous books together) springs from that deep friendship, respect, and creative collaboration that we share, and we appreciate having this opportunity to publicly express our acknowledgment of that mutual respect and camaraderie. Peter: thank you. And George: back at you.

In the next breath, we thank "Stefanie" and all our thousands of other clients, whose experiences, challenges, and triumphs inform the pages of this book and make these principles come to life. In many ways our clients help teach us humility, creativity, and continued awareness of the perseverance of human spirit to overcome even the darkest of challenges. We treasure and deeply respect the trust and confidence that our clients place in us, as they share with us their inner feelings, thoughts, and life experiences and we work together to find the best ways to resolve the problems that bring them to our door.

Our thanks next go to our intrepid coexplorer, John David Mann, who brought to this project boundless enthusiasm, preternatural energy, unflagging humor, and a way with words that can only be described as *magical.* John did more than simply put our approach into words; he helped to fundamentally shape the material and brought crucial insights and structural clarity to it as well. (And we'll reveal a secret here: the "journalist named David" in chapters 1 and 2? That's actually *John David.*) This book would not exist without him.

To Margret McBride, literary agent extraordinaire and the best friend an author could have. Margret saw this project from its earliest germ of a thought to its conclusion in the book you hold in your hands, and was right there with us through thick and thin. It was Margret who found us our coauthor, Margret who found us our publisher, Margret who came up with the book's clever title (with a grateful nod to Schiller and Beethoven), and Margret who believed in us and what we were doing even when there wasn't a single word yet on paper.

To Margret's brilliant and dedicated crew, Faye Atchison, Anne Bomke, and Donna Degutis, who scrutinized portions of the manuscript with expert eyes and helped bring greater clarity to the project when it was in its earliest stages.

To Gideon Weil, our editor, and to Claudia Boutote, Michael Maudlin, Suzanne Quist, Maria Schulman, Mark Tauber, and the rest of the remarkable crew at HarperOne. There are publishers, and then there are publishers: the people at HarperOne are not just a staff but a genuine community, united through their shared devotion both to excellence and to creating books that better the human condition. We need more like you.

To Larry King, for his generous and adventurous spirit, for his taking such a keen interest in our work, and for cheerfully providing this book with its delightful foreword. And to Wendy Walker and Randy Woods, and Allison and Eric Glader, Larry's producers, for their constant and faithful support of our work.

To Debbie Ford, for her constant friendship and inspiration and for helping to bring this whole project about.

To our amazing colleagues, too numerous to catalog here, and especially to Larry Dossey, M.D., David Feinstein, Ph.D., John Freedom, Bessel van der Kolk, M.D., Bruce Lipton, Ph.D., Candace Pert, Ph.D., and Carolyn Sakai, Ph.D.: they are, every last one, not only giants in the field of health and healing but also remarkably compassionate and dedicated people. Larry, David, John, Bessel, Bruce, Candace, Carolyn: the world is an enormously better place for your being here.

To Greg Nicosia, Ph.D., and all the creative and supportive people at the Association for Comprehensive Energy Psychology (ACEP) for helping to create a forum that encourages work like ours. Greg: this book wouldn't exist if we hadn't known you.

Our deepest thanks to Donna J. Kimball at the Material Measurement Laboratory, National Institute of Standards and Technology (NIST); to Stacy Bruss, NIST Librarian; to Teressa Rush-Cover, with NIST's Measurement Services Division; and to Anne Meininger from the National Center for Standards and Certification Information (NCSCI), for their help in chasing down accurate data on the water composition of fog. And likewise to Julio L. Hernandez-Delgado, head of Archives and Special Collections at Hunter College Libraries in New York; Kate Boyle at the Jones Library Special Collections in Amherst, Massachusetts; and Kimberly Baker, librarian at the Scripps Memorial Hospital in La Jolla; for their help in accessing Barbara Kolonay's original master's thesis on the visualizing basketball players.

To Brittany Smith, at the Fred Rogers Company, for her kind assistance in securing permission to use the first stanza of Fred Rogers's timeless song, *What Do You Do with the Mad that You Feel?*

Thanks go to Sally and Whitney Pratt; David and Pat Pratt, Chad Pratt, Erin Osterholm, M.D., and Connor Pratt; Ginger and Darren Allen; Jill Pratt; Karen, David, Audrey, and Grace Pike; Becky, Dan, Jacob, Matthew, and Luke Cinadar; Floyd, Kenny, Sandra, Kyle, and Whitney Prater, for their love and support over the years. Also to Marcia Andrews for her encouragement; Larissa and Brenden Lambrou for their emotional support; Paula Shaw for sharing her astute knowledge of the chakra system; Michael Yapko, Ph.D., for inspiration and focus on people's strengths; George's father, George Pratt, Senior, a constant source of inspiration and role model for treating all people with kindness and living each moment with bottomless humor and a deep appreciation of life; and Peter's mother, Mary Lambrou, who provided unconditional love and wise guidance, and who sadly left this world before seeing this project come to print.

To Kathy and Colt Bagley, Marnie and Howard Barnhorst, Marisa Coon, Leslie Dillahunt, Beth and Stephen Doyne, Ph.D., Rob Dyrdek, Kim Edstrom, Susan Gawlinski, Belinda Hopper, Robert Howes, Errol Korn, M.D., Ann and Mike Kriozere, Mimi and Howard Lupin, Shyla McClanahan, Stephen Metcalfe, Todd Morgan and Rosanna Arquette, Mike Nagle, Sheila Nellis, Susan and David Nethero, Pat and Jeannie Scott, Noni and Drew Senyei, M.D., Robert Stone, Tom Vendetti, Ph.D., Andres Verjan, Alicia Jarrat and Gib Wiggams, and Heather Young, for all the myriad ways you keep us sane, our feet on the ground, and our lives on track, and all with such grace, ease, and humor.

And our thanks, esteem, approbation, love, and endless admiration go last, best, and most to our wives, Vonda Pratt, Dottie Lambrou, and Ana Gabriel Mann, for standing by us, for putting up with all our jokes (even the lame ones), and for being such blessings in our lives and such integral parts of our own personal code to joy.

ABOUT THE AUTHORS

George Pratt, Ph.D., and **Peter Lambrou, Ph.D.,** are licensed clinical psychologists in practice at Scripps Memorial Hospital in La Jolla, California. Both have served as Chairman of Psychology and are on staff at Scripps. They both maintain private practices in La Jolla, specializing in mind-body techniques, psychotherapy, hypnotherapy, and performance enhancement. Dr. Pratt began his full-time clinical practice in 1976; Dr. Lambrou joined the practice in 1987.

Dr. Pratt is a past president of the San Diego Society of Clinical Hypnosis and is a member of numerous professional associations, including the American Psychological Association, the American Society of Clinical Hypnosis (Fellow, Approved Consultant), and the Association for Comprehensive Energy Psychology (Diplomate), and teaches at the University of California, San Diego. He has appeared on television and radio more than a hundred times, including repeat appearances on *Larry King Live* and MTV.

Dr. Lambrou is past president of the American Psychotherapy and Medical Hypnosis Association and is a member of numerous professional associations, including the Association for Psychological Science and the International Academy of Behavioral Medicine, Counseling and Psychotherapy (Diplomate), and he currently serves as an instructor at the University of California, San Diego. He is a frequent speaker at health symposiums, conferences, and corporate events and has appeared on numerous radio and television broadcasts.

Drs. Pratt and Lambrou are coauthors of *Hyper-Performance: The A.I.M. Strategy for Releasing Your Business Potential* and *Instant Emotional Healing: Acupressure for the Emotions*. Dr. Pratt is coauthor of *A Clinical Hypnosis Primer*, and Dr. Lambrou is coauthor of *Self-Hypnosis: The Complete Manual for Health and Self-Change*.

John David Mann is an award-winning author whose titles include the *New York Times* bestseller *Flash Foresight*, the national bestseller *The Go-Giver*, *It's Not About You*, and *Take the Lead: Motivate, Inspire, and Bring Out the Best in Yourself and Everyone Around You*. His writing has earned the Nautilus Book Awards, the Axiom Business Book Awards (Gold Medal), and Taiwan's Golden Book Award for Innovation.

www.codetojoy.com